ARISTOTLE ON THE
CATEGORY OF RELATION

D1300272

Pamela M. Hood

University Press of America,® Inc.
Lanham · Boulder · New York · Toronto · Oxford

Library of Congress Control Number: 2004111484
ISBN 0-7618-3007-3 (paperback : alk. ppr.)

B836
.H66
2004

o 57449125

To my matriarchs Peggy the slave and Rachel the slave.

Contents

Preface

Many philosophers believe that Aristotle does not have, and indeed could not have, a theory of relation, even one that accounts for relations involving two terms, i.e., dyadic relations. Aristotle's logical, metaphysical and ontological views, especially his substance-accident ontology, are seen as restricting Aristotle to only one-place or monadic relations, and prohibiting the logical space for a separate entity, relation, to exist. Hence, Aristotle's conception of relation is perceived to be so divergent from our own that it does not count as a theory of relation at all. I aim to show that the critics are wrong to speak so poorly of Aristotle's account of relation.

I argue that Aristotle's theory has some of the basic features that a theory of relation must have. I begin in Part One by sketching out the critics' charges. I then outline the main features of Aristotle's philosophy that inform his treatment of the category of relation, and briefly survey Aristotle's discussion of relational issues scattered throughout the corpus. Next, I present an exegesis of Aristotle's two central texts on relation, *Categories* 7 and *Metaphysics* V.15, and discuss the various accounts of relational entities or *relatives* therein. In Part Two, I examine two problems. First, I address the problem of how best to interpret Aristotle's relatives. Second, I explore the epistemological difficulties stemming from Aristotle's view in the *Categories* that relation involves two relative items or terms and that if one relative item is known definitely the other item must also be known definitely.

I conclude that Aristotle's treatment of relatives reveals his commitment to the view that there be a dyad, i.e., at least two items, involved in a relation. Furthermore, I show that Aristotle includes in his theory something that accounts for the relation itself, i.e., something approaching a logical relational predicate. I do not suggest that Aristotle attempts to construct a relational theory comparable to our own. But I do suggest that given Aristotle's grasp of the dyadic nature of relation, we have good reason to believe Aristotle's theory of relation is more robust than many suspect.

Acknowledgments

My thanks to colleagues at San Francisco State University and Claremont Graduate University for their help and encouragement during the completion of this manuscript.

Part One: The Exegesis

Chapter 1

Categories 7

1. Introduction

Many scholars think that Aristotle's conception of relation is so different from our own that it does not count as a theory of relation at all. Philosophers complain that his view of relation is inadequate or simply wrong.[1] In this Chapter, I sketch out the critics' charges. I then consider the main features of Aristotle's philosophy that inform his treatment of the category of relation, briefly reviewing Aristotle's discussion of relational issues scattered throughout the corpus.

Aristotle does not have the help of a logical apparatus comparable to that used in modern logic to articulate a relational theory. He relies instead on language.[2] Consequently, there sometimes is no sure way to tell whether Aristotle is using or mentioning a word to signify a metaphysical relational predicate, a relation, a concrete relative item, or simply a relative word. To help distinguish between these, I will adopt the following convention: words that signify a concrete relative item will be left unaltered (e.g., someone who is a slave); relations, metaphysical relational predicates, and relational attributes (or properties) will be underlined (e.g., the relation is a slave of, the metaphysical predicate slave, the property being a slave); and relative words to which Aristotle refers will be placed in single quotes (e.g., 'slave', 'larger'). A look at a relational proposition will help illustrate these conventions. The propositions "Peggy is a slave of Tucker" or "Rachel is a slave of Hill" mention the relation is a slave of, in this case the relation involving my maternal and paternal matriarchs and their masters.[3]

Understanding relations as dyadic is fundamental to the modern logic of relation.[4] First-order logic and set theory are the predominant means used in modern logic to discuss relations. In first-order logic, a relation is a two-place (or more) propositional function (or predicate) that is satisfied (or instantiated) by appropriately ordered items, arguments, or terms. If item a is related by a relation R to item b, this relationship can be shown as R(ab). This can be read in any of several ways: "a is related by R to b," "a has the relation R to b," "a stands in relation R to b," and various other expressions.

We can symbolize the relation as follows: Let 'S' be the relation is a slave of, 'p' be Peggy, and 't' be her master, Tucker. Thus 'S(pt)' symbolizes the relational proposition, "Peggy is a slave of Tucker." Because the order in which the terms are given represents the precise relationship in which the individuals stand, we say that the terms of a relation are *ordered*. For some relations the order in which the terms appear is critical. For instance, the statement "Peggy is a slave of Tucker" becomes false if the terms "Peggy" and "Tucker" are switched: Tucker was not the slave of Peggy. The ordering of terms in some relations, of course, does not affect the relation. The relation is the sibling of is such a case. The sibling relation I have with my brother, Michael, can just as easily be symbolized 'S(pm)' ("Pamela is the sibling of Michael") or 'S(mp)' ("Michael is the sibling of Pamela").

To recap, in first-order logic the logical syntax of relation allows us to specify a relational predicate, the number of items involved in the relation, and their order. From these three features we arrive at two criteria a theory of relation must meet to be on a par with our modern first-order logic. First, it must account for the minimally dyadic, ordered character of relation. Second, it must account for some relational predicate apart from the two items that stand in relation to each other.

Set theory provides another modern approach to understanding relation. Set theory gives us a way of describing collections or sets of things be they basketballs, opera singers, or numbers. With the exception of an empty (or null) set, a set is composed of elements (or members) of the set. As in first-order logic, the terms or elements may be unordered or ordered.

Set theory allows us to describe relations quite easily: A relation is any set of ordered pairs.[5] Take an ordered pair, e.g., (x, y), where 'x' is a slave and 'y' is a master. A set, call it R, of similarly ordered pairs of slaves and their masters defines the relation of being a slave or slavehood:

$$R \quad \{(x_1,y_1), (x_2,y_2), (x_3,y_3), (x_4,y_4), (x_5,y_5), (x_6,y_6), \ldots \}$$

The relationship the first term of each ordered pair has with the second term can be shown as $R(xy)$. This expression can be read as "x stands in relation R to y," and various other ways noted earlier in the discussion of first-order logic.

The standards for what counts as expressing a relational theory are less stringent in set theory than they are for first-order logic. This is because only the first criterion is needed to express adequately the relational theory. The criterion that a relational theory be able to account for the minimally dyadic, ordered character of relation ably captures what constitutes a relation from a set-theoretical point of view. The second criterion, that there be some accounting for a relational predicate apart from the dyad, is not necessary to express what makes set-theory a legitimate relational theory. Meeting the demands of first-order logic, then, is a more stringent task. Since most critics have first-order logic in mind when they criticize Aristotle's relational theory, I, too, shall consider how Aristotle's relational theory stands with respect to both criteria under that approach rather than the set-theoretic approach to relation.

Critics contend Aristotle's logical, ontological, and metaphysical views prohibit him from meeting either of the two criteria. The critics believe Aristotle could not have a theory of relation that accounts for relations involving two terms, i.e., dyadic relations. The most Aristotle can offer, they say, is a discussion of predicational issues surrounding relative words and relational properties. To support their claims, critics regularly point to two central features of Aristotle's philosophy: his substance-accident ontology and his reduction of propositions to the logical structure of subject-predicate form.

The following Sections explore these two fundamental aspects of Aristotle's philosophy. I examine how Aristotle's introduces his metaphysical and ontological view, or "meta-ontology," and category theory in the *Categories*, by briefly describing Aristotle's substance-accident ontology. In addition, I discuss Aristotle's reliance on the reduction of propositions to subject-predicate form and the role this plays in his philosophy of language, logic, and science.

1.1 Aristotle's Meta-ontology

In the *Organon*, Aristotle takes up the study of the elementary units of what exists, how they can be discussed in language, and how to engage in scientific and dialectical reasoning. In the *Categories*, Aristotle presents his meta-ontology by examining the beings (*onta*) that actually exist, the manners in which they exist, and the way in which these are knowable as conceptual units of thought in and through language as "saids" or "sayables" (*legomena*).

Substance (*ousia*) in the *Categories* includes both concrete individuals and secondary substances such as genera and their species. All substances can be subjects, but not all subjects are substances. By 'subject' Aristotle means whatever has anything said of it or in it. That is, a subject is that of which anything else is predicated or in which something inheres.

Aristotle distinguishes two different ways in which one thing can be predicated of another. In one mode, he will say that the predicated item is *said of* its subject: Thus if Frederick is a man, Aristotle will say, "Man is said of Frederick." In the other mode, he will say that the predicated item is *present in, inheres in,* or simply *in* its subject. Thus if Frederick is just, Aristotle will say, "Justice is present in Frederick."

A simple combinatorial exercise involving these two modes of predication generates a classification of what there is. According to *Categories* 1a20–b8, there are four types of beings or *onta*. (Type-1) Some things are said of a subject (*hupokeimenon*) but do not inhere in a subject. For instance, man, i.e., the species *Homo sapiens*, is said of persons, but the species man does not inhere in anything. (Type-2) Some things inhere in a subject but are not said of a subject. According to *Categories* 1a23–25, a Type-2 item is an item that is in a subject but not in that subject as a part of the subject. Rather, the item is something that is in the subject and cannot exist separately from its subject. For instance, individual knowledge, e.g., a particular piece of grammatical knowledge, say, my knowledge that plural subjects take plural verbs, is in my soul (*psyche*), but individual knowledge is not said of any subject. (Type-3) Some things are both said of and inhere in a subject. Color is said of pallor, Aristotle thinks, since pallor is a color; color also inheres in any pale person. (Type-4) Some things are neither said of nor inhere in a subject. An individual man, Nathan, for example, does not inhere in anything nor is he said of anything.

1.2 Aristotle's Category Theory

At *Categories* 1b25-2a3 Aristotle lists ten conceptual thought units or "sayables" (*legomena*), each signifying what have come to be called one of the ten *predicaments* or *categories* (*katêgoriai*) of beings. The ten are: substance (e.g., man or a horse), quantity (e.g., six feet), quality (e.g., the color turquoise), relation (e.g., double or larger), place (e.g., in Hollywood), time (e.g., last year), position (e.g., sitting), having (e.g., has-shoes-on), doing (e.g., burning), or affection (e.g., being-burned). While it may appear that the number of beings or *onta* in the Aristotelian metaphysical panoply are increasing, there are not now *fourteen* sorts of *onta*. Aristotle identifies the same *onta* in two different ways. The first is in terms of the ontological and logical relationships all beings have, or do not have, with each other. Some *onta* have the logical relationship of being said of a subject, other *onta* have the ontological relationship of actually inhering in a subject. In the category of substance, for example, primary substance is a Type-4 being (no primary substance is said of or inheres in anything); secondary substance is a Type-1 being (the genus animal is said of a subject, but it does not inhere in any subject). Second, beings are identified in terms of the category to which that being belongs. The beings in the categories listed here at *Categories* 1b25 and the beings Aristotle divides into four types at 1a20, then, overlap. That is, the two lists of *onta* are co-extensive in that all the entities in the ten categories correspond to at least one of the four types of *onta*.

Starting at *Categories* 5, Aristotle proceeds to discuss the characteristics of substance (*ousia*) and makes a paradigmatic distinction between substances and the nine categories of non-substances. There are two kinds of substances: primary substances (e.g., an individual person or horse), the things Aristotle considers actual or concrete entities, and secondary substances (e.g., a genus or species such as animal or *Homo sapiens*), which indicate what kind of thing a substance is.

Aristotle orients his ontology and his theory of predication toward primary substance. He says that everything save primary substances (i.e., secondary and non-substantial entities) are predicated of primary substances as subjects or are in them as subjects (*Categories* 2a34). According to *Categories* 2a36–2b1, if none of the things that are predicated of secondary substances, i.e., the genera and species of things, were not in fact predicated of individuals in those genera and species, no secondary substances could be predicated of anything at all. As Aristotle conceives of it, we can say that color is in body because color is in an individual body. If red were not in *some* body, e.g., if red were not in this ball or some other primary substance, then red would not be in a body at all (*Categories* 2b1–3). So if it were not for primary substance, none of the other *onta*—neither secondary substances, nor qualities, quantities, relatives, and so forth—would exist (*Categories* 2a35). Thus, for Aristotle, everything (except for primary substances) depends on primary substance.

We see, then, that Aristotle describes two predicative relationships among beings: (1) the relationship of being *said of* some thing and (2) the relationship of *inhering in* some thing. The former Aristotle uses to signify either the relationship of a universal to a particular, or the relationship of a genus to a species. Throughout I will I treat a universal as something equivalent to a metaphysical predicate. I will say, then, that a universal or a metaphysical predicate, for example, man, musical, slave, is something that can be predicated of a number of things, while a particular is an item that is an individual, for example, Socrates or Peggy (*De Interpretatione* 17a39–17b1, see also *Metaphysics* 1038b10–12). Aristotle uses the latter relationship of inherence to note the relationship of an individual attribute and the particular thing that has the attribute. For Aristotle, no universal exists uninstantiated; that is, universals do not have a separate existence the way in which Plato's Forms do. (See *Categories* 2a34–35, 2b3–6, and 14a7–10. For Aristotle's criticism of the Platonists' separation of universals see, e.g., *Metaphysics* 1078b9–1080a10 and *Metaphysics* 1087a30–b12).

From *Categories* 6 on, Aristotle discusses the categories of non-substantial entities. Non-substantial entities are attributes that a thing has, for example, such things as qualities, quantities, relatives, and their genera. These are commonly called *accidents* or *properties*, and although the two expressions nowadays are often used synonymously, each has its own technical use in Aristotle. A property for Aristotle is something that a thing has that is not stated in the definition of a thing, but nonetheless follows from that thing's nature (see *Topics* 101b19–23 and 102a18–30). For instance, the ability to learn a language is a property of human beings, but it is not in the definition of a human being. An accident, on the other hand, is neither a property of a thing nor part of its definition, but rather is a feature that belongs to a subject but not necessarily so. An accident, therefore, is something contingent or incidental to its underlying subject. Addell's being in Hot Springs or being six feet tall is something incidental to her being human, for she might just as well be in Los Angeles or Lubbock, or be five feet nine inches tall or six feet two inches tall.

Despite the fact that all entities in the non-substantial categories share this common feature of being able to be contingent entities, strictly speaking, each of these categories is metaphysically unique in that it represents a distinctive kind of being.[6] What it is to be in Paris, for example, is different from what it is to be wearing Ferragamo shoes or to be six feet tall. Part of what Aristotle does with his category theory, then, is to prescribe the boundaries, or what I call the *categorial integrity*, of each of the categories.

Relatives, though, are especially different from all the other categories, and the substance-accident paradigm is key to understanding why this is so. All non-substantial entities rely on substance for their existence, but in addition, relatives rely on non-substantial entities in other categories for the ground of their existence. This makes them "posterior" to the entities in those categories, and hence in Aristotle's opinion, just that much more removed from substance. This is why Aristotle places relatives at the extreme end of non-substantial being, calling them the "least real" and most dependent of all entities:

> the relative is least of all things a real thing or substance, and is posterior to quality and quantity; and the relatives are accidents of quantity . . . but not its matter, since there is something else both for relative in general and for its parts and kinds. For there is nothing either great or small, many or few, or, in general, relative, which is many or few, great or small, or relative without being so as something else. (*Metaphysics* 1088a24–29, see also *Nicomachean Ethics* 1096a19)[7]

Aristotle discusses two important features of relatives in this passage. First, whatever is relative exists as some other thing first. When Aristotle says here that there is nothing many or few, for example, without being so as something else, he means that whatever 'few' signifies, it must be a few *something*: a few burgers, bicycles or books. A relative cannot be a relative all by itself, as it were.

Second, Aristotle describes how it is that relatives rely on other entities for their existence. The example he has in mind is something like the following. Take two things, say, pencil A and pencil B; one pencil is 5 inches long, the other 6 inches. What makes pencil A shorter than pencil B, is pencil A's length being less than the length of pencil B. Length falls under the category of quantity, and quantity is an accident of substance. So in this case at least, being relative means being dependent upon an accident in another category. It is this characteristic that makes relatives such dependent entities and so different from substance, and from primary substance in particular, which is not dependent on any other entity.

Now as no relative can exist without its having its own ground and support (e.g., pencil A's existence and its having a certain length), there cannot be a relative without another item, in this case, pencil B which has a length longer than the 5 inches of pencil A. The relation is shorter than clearly is something that involves two items. While this seems an extremely obvious point to make, it is a point, say Aristotle's critics, he has difficulty making. The difficulty stems from Aristotle's being limited, they believe, to only the monadic, one-termed relations of an accident or predicate and *its* subject. The relation is shorter than requires two items, but it is generally believed that Aristotle cannot account for an accident and its relationship to two subjects.

Weinberg remarks that relations cannot be accidents because accidents are one-termed, not the minimally two-termed predicates which relations need to be. Weinberg says that given Aristotle's ontology,

> relation, as accident or affection (πάθος) of substance, exists in primary substance. Moreover, because relation is an accident, it belongs to a single primary substance or to an accident of such a substance. Nowhere is there any suggestion that a relation belongs to two substances taken together in a pair. (Weinberg 1965, 69)

Weinberg reiterates the not-undisputed claim that Aristotle's ontology limits him from conceiving of one accident inhering or being predicated of more than one thing at a time (Weinberg 1965, 75).[8] On Weinberg's view, since Aristotle can regard relatives only as accidents of substance, even if a relational accident were in some sense a relation, the relation *qua* accident would inhere or exist in only one item (the subject), and not a dyad of two items. Thus, if the relation is a slave of is like any other Aristotelian accident, it will only involve one item

(Peggy), not the two items or terms (Peggy and Tucker) necessary for a dyadic relation. Weinberg 1965, 62 also makes the point that no reduction of polyadic to monadic predicates is possible. For a proof that dyadic relations cannot be reduced to monadic ones, Weinberg directs the reader to Lewis and Langford 1932, 387–388. Briefly, Lewis and Langford observe that most attempts to reduce dyadic relations to monadic ones begin by defining a set of dyadic properties (or predicates) and replacing them with a truth-function constructed out of simple monadic predicates, formulating the same dyadic properties on these properties. That is, a set of dyadic properties is defined as $g(x, y)$ in terms of a conjunction of functions with one variable each, e.g., $f'(x)$ & $f''(y)$. The proof that dyadic properties cannot be formulated on monadic ones is that every sentence of the monadic predicate calculus, if satisfiable at all, is satisfiable in some finite model. However, there are sentences of the dyadic predicate calculus that are satisfiable but not satisfiable in any finite model. If we were to make $g(x, y)$ equivalent to a truth-function such as $f'(x)$ & $f''(y)$, then the set defining a non-finite series, i.e., a model satisfiable in the dyadic predicate calculus, would be self-contradictory. Therefore, the force of the dyadic predicate cannot be formulated on a monadic one.

Cornford 1957, 284 similarly contends that Aristotle cannot have an accurate understanding of relation. He maintains that Aristotle only conceives of them as names or things, not relations between things.

> A man has the property 'fatherhood' towards his son. It was reserved for still living logicians to discover that a proposition like 'Socrates is shorter than Phaedo' has two subjects with a relation between them, and no predicate at all. (Cornford 1957, 283)

Although Cornford acknowledges that Aristotle's relational properties are peculiar in that relatives have a reference to something else, he believes Aristotle's relatives are just nouns or adjectives that Aristotle uses as predicates to signify properties.

Other commentators, though, e.g., Cavarnos 1975, think Aristotle does take up relations themselves as well as relational attributes, relational words, and the concrete relative items which serve as the terms of relations. Cavarnos states that

> [Aristotle] uses the term *to pros ti* to refer both to relation and to the thing which has a relation, he is acting in the same way as when he uses the word *ousia* to refer both to the form of a thing and to the thing which is a concretion of form and matter. (Cavarnos 1975, 45)

But Russell would have seen in this account by Cavarnos evidence for why Aristotle's conception of relation is unsatisfactory.

> Traditional logic, since it holds that all propositions have the subject-predicate form, is unable to admit of the reality of relations: all relations, it maintains, must be reduced to properties of the apparently related terms. (Russell 1914, 56)

Asymmetrical relations, Russell says, cannot be reduced to predications of properties. Take, for example, the asymmetrical relation of is bigger than: A is bigger than B, but B is not bigger than A. What we have on the predicational view, Russell says, is simply the predication of "is bigger than" of one of the terms. Thus, as Russell sees it, the difference between Aristotle's theory and ours is that of describing the properties that things have versus describing the relation in which things stand with each other.

Russell does make an exception to his pronouncement, however. The exception is with symmetrical relations, for instance, relations of equality and inequality where if A is equal to B, then B is equal to A, or if C is unequal to D, then D is unequal to C. Russell admits that these kinds of relations can be analyzed as a property two things share. So, saying that A is equal to B, is saying that A and B possess a common property, e.g., that of being 6 feet tall. But even with the relation of inequality, all the predicational view of relations can show is that A and B posses different properties, i.e., all it shows is that A and B are "merely unequal" without indicating which is greater or lesser.

We have seen that Aristotle's metaphysical and ontological views, especially his substance-accident ontology, leads philosophers to think that Aristotle cannot possibly provide a dyadic account of relation. The criticism seems irrefutable. In Aristotle's substance-accident ontology, everything save primary substance is in or is said of primary substance. This means, for example, that an apple's redness inheres in the apple, my being 5'9" inheres in me, and a pencil's shortness, i.e., its being shorter than, inheres in the one pencil. There seems to be no way, given Aristotle's ontology and category theory, for him to go beyond talk of a subject and its relational property (i.e., to present anything other than a monadic account of relation) much less for him to identify something akin to a relation that allows him to articulate the simple dyadic relation of one thing's being shorter than another thing.

1.3 Aristotle's Philosophy of Language, Logic, and Science

As problematic as Aristotle's substance-accident ontology appears to be for his relational theory, so, too, is the next stumbling block: Aristotle's reduction of propositions to a subject-predicate logical form. This reduction is a central element in Aristotle's philosophy of language, logic, and in his guidelines for scientific reasoning.

Aristotle is famous for developing the first systematic treatment of logical inference: his syllogistic. Aristotle's logic rests on the foundation of his philosophy of language. The building blocks of his philosophy of language are names and verbs, which serve as the subjects and predicates of propositions or statements. When names are said without combination (e.g., 'man,' 'runs'), they are neither true nor false, but once said in combination, i.e., once they are joined in a statement or proposition as subject and predicate (e.g., "man runs"), they do have truth values (*Categories* 2a4-10, *De Interpretatione* 16a9–18).

Aristotle believes that all simple statements are composed of names that signify universals or particulars and that either affirm or deny something of a subject. A statement may affirmatively predicate something of a particular, as in the following three statements:

(1) Nathan is a man
(2) Man is said of Nathan
(3) Nathan is musical

In (1) and (2), being human is predicated and affirmed of an individual item, Nathan. In (3), the attribute of being musical is predicated of an individual item. Statements may also deny something of a subject as in, e.g., "Nathan is not a man," "Nathan is not musical," and so forth.[9] In *De Interpretatione* 18a13 ff., Aristotle discusses what it means for a statement to constitute a single affirmation. A statement constitutes a single affirmation when it signifies one thing, or a unity, about one thing. The subjects and predicates in statements (1)-(3) above each represent a single thing, i.e., a unity of some kind: Nathan is a unity because he is one thing; being musical is a unity, because it signifies one thing. According to Aristotle's philosophy of language, the statement

(1) Nathan is a man

has the subject-predicate surface structure of S is P, where one thing, the predicate <u>man</u>, is affirmed of one thing, the subject, Nathan. In modern logic, proposition (1) can be written "Mn", where "M" is a monadic predicate and "n" is an individual constant designating Nathan and where the entire proposition is a substitution instance of the propositional function, $F(x)$. However, given what we have just discussed, when we try to analyze relational statements as one supposes Aristotle would, we run into tremendous difficulties. Here is what I mean. Given the restrictions of both Aristotle's ontology and philosophy of language, the statement:

(4) Peggy is brown

and

(5) Peggy is a slave

appear to have the same surface structure as (1) and warrant the same logical analysis, $F(x)$.

Note that (5) affirms one thing of one thing: It affirms the metaphysical predicate <u>slave</u> of Peggy. There is nothing in the logical form of (5) to account for the other term needed to reflect the dyadic nature of the relation ". . . is a slave of _____." It might be suggested that Aristotle would have half a chance if we restate (5) as:

(6) Peggy is a slave of Tucker.

But the problem continues, or in fact, becomes worse.

If Aristotle is to be consistent in his views, he must say that (6) affirms one thing of one thing. This puts Aristotle in a real bind. He seems to have two options: First, he might treat what is in the predicate position ('is a slave of Tucker') strictly as one complete unity. Or second, he might treat the statement (6) as some sort of combination of these two statements:

(7) Peggy is Tucker's slave

(8) Tucker is Peggy's master

where the two predicates "_____ is Tucker's slave" and "_____ is Peggy's master" each somehow signify one thing.

Aristotle does recognize complex propositions (a) that affirm (or deny) something of two other things (e.g., '*A* and *B* are *C*') or (b) that join two simple propositions together (e.g., '*A* is *C* and *B* is *C*'), but he reduces both to the form '*S* is *P*'. The latter case, he says, just represents a compound version of this simple subject-predicate form, i.e., '*A* is *C*' and '*B* is *C*'. Thus, to say that "Apples *and* oranges are fruits" does not involve any predication other than predicating something of one group of things.

Aristotle does comment (*De Interpretatione* 18a18-27) upon a maneuver not completely unlike option (b) above. Let us take a moment to examine this case.

What option (b) tries to do is find a way around making only one affirmation of one thing at a time. Aristotle sees through the ploy, however. He says that "if one name is given to things which do not make up one thing, there is not a single affirmation" (*De Interpretatione* 18a18, trans. Ackrill). The example he offers is that of giving the word 'cloak' two significations: horse and man. The statement 'a cloak is white' is:

> no different from saying a horse is white and a man is white. So if this last signifies more than one thing and is more than one affirmation, clearly the first also signifies either more than one thing or nothing (because no man is a horse). (*De Interpretatione* 18a22-27)

So, even if we tried to find some name, say, 'tuckerchattel', that somehow could signify two of the logical terms we need (master and slave), the resulting statement—"Peggy is tuckerchattel"—would either just be nonsense ("Peggy is a master") or would simply be reducible to two statements affirming (or denying) one thing of one thing ("Peggy is a master and Peggy is a slave"). In any event, neither option (a) nor (b) have the logical form of the sort modern relational logic accepts, and neither constitutes a *well-formed proposition* of the sort Aristotle requires.

The critics think Aristotle must treat (6) as he does (1): one thing being predicated of one thing, in which case there is no sense of a dyadic relation to be had. On the other hand, if we want to press the issue, and have Aristotle say that the predicate ("is a slave of Tucker") must signify two things, we shall have forced Aristotle to violate a basic component not only of his philosophy of language, but his logic and science as well.

Aristotle's logic is syllogistic. His definition of a valid argument is a "discourse in which, certain things being said, something other than what is stated follows of necessity from their being so" (*Prior Analytics* 24b18). Aristotle thought that the validity of all valid arguments could be demonstrated by (a) translating them into some equivalent syllogism or syllogisms and (b) demonstrating the validity of the resulting syllogisms. A syllogism is composed of categorical statements. Categorical statements affirm (or deny) a predicate of a subject just as singular statements do, but categorical statements differ from singular statements by having *universal* subjects and predicates. Instead of signifying particulars such as Nathan or Ella, universal subjects signify general terms such as mammal, cows, or dogs. Predications involving universal statements differ in *quantity*. For example, either the predicate is affirmed of all of the subject ("Every dog is a mammal"), affirmed of none of the subject ("No cows are dogs"), affirmed of some of the subject ("Some men are musical"), or denied of some of the subject ("Some mammals are not musical"). With categorical statements it may appear that Aristotle affirms (or denies) more than one thing of more than one other thing. But when he says, for example, that "All cows are mammals," he still is affirming something (being a mammal) of something (the totality of all cows).

The syllogism has three categorical propositions, two premises and a conclusion, each of which attributes something of some subject. The inference from the two premises leads to a conclusion that establishes one thing of some thing (*Prior Analytics* 40b23, 41a5). A syllogism is valid if there is a necessary relation between the terms of the conclusion based on both terms' relation to a common third (or "middle") term. Aristotle devised configurations or figures of syllogisms that dictate how the three terms may be combined. The first figure, for example, produces the familiar, valid argument form: All A's are B's; all B's are C's; therefore, all A's are C's.

Lastly, I want to mention, briefly, the relationship between the foregoing and Aristotle's philosophy of science. Science, for Aristotle, consists of a body of knowledge about a particular subject matter; however, the body of knowledge is not just an assemblage of facts about a subject. Aristotle believes that to have scientific knowledge is to understand the cause of something, i.e., to have the explanation of why a thing is the way it is. The way we arrive at these explanations is through demonstration (*Posterior Analytics* I.2).

In short, a demonstration is a deduction from true premises that themselves can be grasped without demonstration. The inferences drawn from these premises lead to a necessarily true conclusion. In demonstrations, the cause (i.e., the explanation of why something is so) appears in the third or middle term. Aristotle gives an example in *Posterior Analytics* 98b5-10. Let *A* be the property of shedding its leaves, *B* the property of being a broad-leaved plant, and *C* the property of being a vine. If *A* belongs to *B*, and *B* belongs to *C*, then *A* belongs to *C*. The argument, then, is as follows: Broad-leaved plants shed their leaves. Vines are broad-leaved plants. Therefore, vines shed their leaves. *B*, the middle term, explains why vines shed their leaves. Demonstrations show the necessary relationship of one thing belonging, or being attributable, to some thing, but because accidents are contingent entities with respect to substances (*Posterior Analytics* 75a19-20). Thus one wonders, if relations are accidents and accidents are contingent with respect to substances, how can there be a logic, i.e., a *necessary* science of relational accidents?

In the past few Sections, I have reviewed reasons in support of the predominant view that Aristotle could not have a legitimately dyadic conception of relation. The basic features of Aristotle's ontology are seen as restricting Aristotle to only one-place or monadic relations, and prohibiting the logical space for a separate entity, relation, to exist. Furthermore, since Aristotle thinks that propositions assert one thing of something, it seems next to impossible for him to articulate a theory of predication that would allow him to assert something of more than one thing. Moreover, we have seen how easily Aristotle's philosophy of language, logic, and science hamper his development of an actual *logic* of relation.

Although the evidence against him is daunting, I think it a disservice to accept the critics' charges so readily. While it is true that Aristotle never developed a logic of relation, and had no formal way of articulating his conception of relation, he nevertheless addressed the topic of relation and explored relational issues throughout the corpus.

1.4 Treatment of Relation in the Corpus

Categories 7 and its sister text, *Metaphysics* V.15, are devoted entirely to the category of relation and the examination of relatives or relational entities. *Categories* 7 and *Metaphysics* V.15 are each a kind of philosophical primer—the *Categories* an ontological; *Metaphysics* V.15 a philosophical lexicon—where Aristotle explains how relative words, the concepts they convey, and the realities they express are understood. These two texts represent Aristotle's most thorough treatment of the topic. The reader, however, supposing that a chapter on relation in both the *Categories* and the *Metaphysics* is devoted to relation alone, should be aware that Aristotle does not have a separate technical word for "relative" and "relation." He uses the term *pros ti*—literally, "toward something" or "in relation to something"—for both, and so it is not always clear exactly what Aristotle has in mind in his discussions. Consequently, we must rely on context to help determine which Aristotle means. Sometimes he appears to treat relational entities as words; sometimes as metaphysical and linguistic predicates; sometimes as logical terms or concrete entities; sometimes as relations. For the time being, I will refer to Aristotle's "*pros ti*" entities as "relational entities," "relational beings," or simply "relatives." I believe that using these expressions broadly at first will allow for flexibility in interpreting the texts without prejudicing a more exact use of these and other expressions later on for the various kinds of relational issues that emerge in both the *Categories* and the *Metaphysics*.

Apart from texts devoted to relation, Aristotle almost always mentions relational being in his many lists or examples of different kinds of being. An exception is *De Anima* 402a23-25. The *Categories* is itself one such list. In addition, see *Topics* 103b21-23, 152a38-39; *Posterior Analytics* 83a21-23, 83b13-17; *Physics* 190a33-35, 225b5-9; *Metaphysics* 1017a24-27; and *Nicomachean Ethics* 1096a23-29.

Furthermore, Aristotle relies on the concept of relation to articulate his views about things distinct from relation. In the *Categories* chapter on quantity, for instance, Aristotle says that lines, planes, and bodies, are distinguished by the positions they have relative to each other (*Categories* 5a15-22, see also *Physics* 208b23-24). He also describes the parts of time as having a relative order, with one part of time being before or after another part of time (5a23-29). Though Aristotle sometimes considers position as a separate category in its own right (*Categories* 1b25-27, *Topics* 103b21-23), he includes it in the category of relation at *Categories* 6b2-6.

Russell and Whitehead 1927 mention De Morgan's supposed comment that Aristotle could not prove that, because a horse is an animal, the head of the horse is the head of an animal.[10] But, although Aristotle cannot prove them, he does seem to have recognized instances of just this relational inference. According to *Topics* 114a18:

> if knowledge is a belief, then the object of knowledge is also an object of belief; and if sight is a perception, then the object of sight is also an object of perception. (See also *Topics* 119b3)

Relational issues also appear in Aristotle's discussion of dialectic and argumentation in *Topics* VI. There he remarks that since being relative is being in a certain relation to something else, when one defines a relative one must mention the relative's *correlative* (see *Topics* 142a28-31, 146b3-4).[11] That is, one cannot define <u>double</u> without reference to what the double is double of, namely, <u>half</u>.

Modern relational theory classifies relations in many ways according to the specific properties a relation has. There are four main properties relations may have, and Aristotle uses or discusses all of them: (i) reflexivity, which concerns the relationship a term has to itself, (ii) symmetry, which concerns the ordering of the terms, and (iii) transitivity, which concerns two-termed relations carrying across a middle term. Relations also are classified according to (iv) the number of terms they have: monadic (one term), dyadic (two terms), and polyadic (two or more terms). What follows is a short survey of the kinds of relations and their characteristics Aristotle utilizes or discusses.[12]

Relational Reflexivity

A reflexive relation is a relation that each thing bears to itself. A relation is reflexive, then, *iff*, for all x, x is related by R to x. For example, "is the same age as" or "is as tall as" are reflexive relations. For any given person, she will be the same age as herself. Aristotle considers sameness a unity and within this context develops views on sameness relations. A sameness relation results, for Aristotle, when one thing is the same as some other thing (*Topics* I.7, VII.1; see also *Metaphysics* V.9) or when one thing is related to itself, Aristotle says, as "when (one thing) is treated as more than one, i.e., when we say a thing is the same as itself; for we treat it as two" (*Metaphysics* 1018a7-9, trans. Ross). Here Aristotle is thinking of sameness relations as also being reflexive because every thing bears an sameness relation to itself.

Relational Symmetry

(a) Symmetrical relations. A relation R is symmetrical *iff*, for all x and for all y, if x is related by R to y, then y is also related by R to x. At *Metaphysics* V.15, Aristotle considers <u>equality</u> a symmetrical relation (*Metaphysics* 1021b6–8).

(b) Asymmetrical relations. A relation R is asymmetrical *iff*, for all *x* and for all *y*, if *x* is related by R to *y*, then *y* is not related by R to *x*. For instance, is the parent of and is louder than are asymmetrical relations. If Lily is the parent of her daughter Bernice, then Bernice is not the parent of Lily. Aristotle discusses the asymmetrical relation between the unmoved mover to other things (*Metaphysics* 1072b2–30). The relations are asymmetrical because the unmoved mover originates movement towards itself but other things do not originate movement of the unmoved mover to themselves. Aristotle also treats intentional relations as thinking and perception as asymmetrical (see *Categories* 7 and *Metaphysics* V.15). Thinking is asymmetrical, for example, because there are instances in which *A* thinks of *B* but *B* does not think of *A*.

Relational Transitivity

Moreover, Aristotle even appears to have a notion of transitive relations. A relation R is transitive *iff*, for all *x*, *y*, and *z*, if *x* is related by R to *y* and *y* is related by R to *z*, then *x* is related by R to *z*. For example, is taller than is transitive because if *A* is taller than *B*, and *B* is taller than *C*, *A* is taller than *C*. Later in the *Topics*, he describes a transitive sameness relationship involving terms:

> Again, look and see if whether the one to be the same as something, the other also is the same as it; for if they are not both the same as the same thing, clearly neither are they the same as one another. (*Topics* 152a31–32, trans. Ross)

Aristotle has in mind the following: If *A* is the same as *C*, and *B* is not the same as *C*, then *A* is not the same as *B*.

Polyadic Relations

Aristotle treats many pairs of relatives (e.g., slave and master, double and half), as dyadic relations such as is a slave of or is double of. Aristotle also treats is a friend of as a relation involving two items. At *Nicomachean Ethics* VIII Aristotle considers the forms and causes of friendship, characterizing it as a relationship between pairs of individuals, countrymen, states, monarchs and their subjects, spouses, parents and their children, and siblings (see *Nicomachean Ethics* 1156b24, 1161a10–11, 1161b11–1162a5).

Aristotle also discusses and utilizes relations with three or more terms. Examples of polyadic relations are is transferring something to or is obtaining a loan from. These are *triadic* relations because they involve three terms, say, Bernice, car, and Pamela: *Bernice* is transferring a *car* to *Pamela*. Aristotle's discussion of gift-giving at *Topics* 125a16–18 is another example of his employment of a three-termed relation (see Morales 1994, 270). Although Aristotle does not explicitly state that someone, say, person *A*, is doing the transferring, his point, nevertheless, is that a transfer (or a gift) is "a transfer (*by someone*) of something and to someone" (italics mine). That is, the transfer is "of something," say, *B*, from someone, say, *A*, and "to someone," say *C*. Thus, the idea he means to convey is that *A* transfers *B* to *C*. Last, Aristotle describes distributive justice as involving a kind of a proportion or ratio that involves the clearly polyadic relation of four terms: two for the people and two for the matter involved in the manifestation of justice. At *Nicomachean Ethics* 1131a15–24 Aristotle says

> [t]he just, therefore, involves at least four terms; the persons for whom it is in fact just are two, and the things in which it is evident, i.e., the objects, are two. The same equality will exist between the persons and between the things concerned; for as the latter—the things concerned—are related, so are the former; if they are not equal, they will not have what is equal, however this is the origin of quarrels and complaints—when either equals have and are awarded unequal shares, or unequals equal shares. (See also *Nicomachean Ethics* 1131b3-4)

As even this brief survey shows, it is clear that Aristotle utilized and discussed relation and features of relations in the corpus. But given the limitations of some of Aristotle's fundamental philosophical views, the question is: just how well and to what degree could he have had a conception of dyadic relation?

Chapter 2

Categories 7

Aristotle's task in *Categories* 7 is no different from the task he faces elsewhere in regard to other categories: to circumscribe the metaphysical and ontological boundaries of each category. He must find a way to delimit the kinds of things that can be included in the category of relation. To accomplish this, he must give an account of what it means to be relational; that is, he must give an account that provides the metaphysical and ontological conditions for *relational* as opposed to other sorts of being. Aristotle's achieving this objective depends on his varied and cumulative efforts in noticing how language, epistemology, and ontology inform our understanding of relation.

2. Aristotle's First Account of Relatives

Aristotle gives two clearly different accounts of relational being in the *Categories*. For the first account, he gives us a preliminary definition of relational being, which is followed by four sets of examples. Aristotle's preliminary definition appears at *Categories* 6a36–37:

> Such things are called *(legetai)* relative to something *(pros ti)* as are said to be the very things they are *of other* things *(heterôn)* or in some other way are said *(legetai)* to be relative to *(pros)* another *(heteron)* thing.

All things, then, are called relative which are just what they are
of something else or are in some manner *toward* another thing.

Aristotle states at *Categories* 8a29 and 8a33 that L is a definition of
relatives, although strictly speaking, it is not a "definition." According
to *Topics* 103b15, a definition consists of genus and differentia. To give
a definition here, Aristotle would need to give the genus plus the
differentia of *pros ti*. This is impossible to do since each category
represents a highest genus of being. None of the categories, therefore,
can be defined with respect to both a genus and a difference.

    L echoes Plato's own distinction between absolute being and
relational being, i.e., between a thing in itself *(kath' hauto)* and a thing
relative to something else *(pros allo)* (see *Sophist* 255c12–13). Indeed,
early commentators on the *Categories* note that Aristotle owes this
formulation to Plato.[13] (For more of the general way Aristotle conceives
of relatives referring to other items, see, for example, *Topics* 142a28–30
and *Sophistical Refutations* 173b1–5.)

2.1 The Four Sets of Examples

We can grasp to some extent what Aristotle considers a relational entity
by examining the four sets of examples of relatives he gives starting at
Categories 6a38, 6b2, 6b6, and 6b11. The point of each set of examples
is to show that relatives are L-compliant because they are always
spoken of with reference to something.

    For the first set of examples, Aristotle gives the following:

> The larger is called just what it is *than* something (for it is called <u>larger
> than</u> something); and what is double is called just what it is *of*
> something else (for it is called <u>double of</u> something), and similarly with
> other things such as these. (*Categories* 6a38–b2)

This first set of examples shows that L relatives belong in the category
of relation because they are always spoken of in comparison to other
things. For example, we say a bowl of ice cream is the double *of* a bowl
with half as much ice cream or that Mount Baldy is larger *than* some
other thing, such as the Huntington Library.

    For his second cluster of examples, Aristotle says:

> And these kinds of things are among the relatives also, e.g., <u>state,
> condition, perception, knowledge, position</u>. For each of the items

All things, then, are called relative which are just what they are
of something else or are in some manner *toward* another thing.

Aristotle states at *Categories* 8a29 and 8a33 that *L* is a definition of
relatives, although strictly speaking, it is not a "definition." According
to *Topics* 103b15, a definition consists of genus and differentia. To give
a definition here, Aristotle would need to give the genus plus the
differentia of *pros ti*. This is impossible to do since each category
represents a highest genus of being. None of the categories, therefore,
can be defined with respect to both a genus and a difference.

 L echoes Plato's own distinction between absolute being and
relational being, i.e., between a thing in itself *(kath' hauto)* and a thing
relative to something else *(pros allo)* (see *Sophist* 255c12–13). Indeed,
early commentators on the *Categories* note that Aristotle owes this
formulation to Plato.[13] (For more of the general way Aristotle conceives
of relatives referring to other items, see, for example, *Topics* 142a28–30
and *Sophistical Refutations* 173b1–5.)

2.1 The Four Sets of Examples

We can grasp to some extent what Aristotle considers a relational entity
by examining the four sets of examples of relatives he gives starting at
Categories 6a38, 6b2, 6b6, and 6b11. The point of each set of examples
is to show that relatives are *L*-compliant because they are always
spoken of with reference to something.

 For the first set of examples, Aristotle gives the following:

> The larger is called just what it is *than* something (for it is called <u>larger
> than</u> something); and what is double is called just what it is *of*
> something else (for it is called <u>double of</u> something), and similarly with
> other things such as these. (*Categories* 6a38–b2)

This first set of examples shows that *L* relatives belong in the category
of relation because they are always spoken of in comparison to other
things. For example, we say a bowl of ice cream is the double *of* a bowl
with half as much ice cream or that Mount Baldy is larger *than* some
other thing, such as the Huntington Library.

 For his second cluster of examples, Aristotle says:

> And these kinds of things are among the relatives also, e.g., <u>state,
> condition, perception, knowledge, position</u>. For each of the items

mentioned is called what it is (and not something else) *of* other things. (*Categories* 6b2)

Aristotle later addresses some peculiarities with several of these relatives (*Categories* 6b11–12, 7b25–8a12). For now, however, let us note three things about this second cluster.

First, note that all the relatives listed are genera, each of which Aristotle takes to be *L*-compliant. However, at *Categories* 8, Aristotle makes the point that genera are often relatives even though particular cases of them are not (*Categories* 11a20). Aristotle reasons that knowledge is relative because it is always knowledge *of* something (e.g., of grammar) but that a particular kind of knowledge (e.g., grammatical knowledge) is not relative because it is not *of* something (e.g., grammatical knowledge is not grammar *of* something) (see *Categories* 11a24–31).

Second, we see that some of the relatives Aristotle mentions are genera belonging to other categories. He says that <u>state</u> and <u>condition</u> are relatives but that the particular cases of them are not relatives (*Categories* 11a20–24). <u>State</u> and <u>condition</u> are said with reference to something; this feature allows them to be included in the category of relation. However, because <u>state</u> and <u>condition</u> are things in virtue of which something is said to be qualified somehow, they also can be included in the category of quality. At *Categories* 11a37–38, Aristotle reassures us that if something were to be both a quality and a relative, it could belong to both categories. At other places, he warns against mistaking things in other categories as relatives simply on the basis of whether two things are somehow related to, or stand in some relation to, each other. At *Categories* 12b16, for instance, after stating that privation and possession are opposed to one another, Aristotle says that these are not opposed to one another in the manner in which correlatively reciprocal relatives are.

The third, and most important, thing to note is that with these examples at *Categories* 6b2, and with *L* in general, Aristotle emphasizes how grammatical features of relatives reveal the characteristic that all relatives share: their always being said in relation to something. States and conditions are qualities. Qualities are qualifications or modifications that subjects possess. So, for Aristotle, when someone is healthy or someone is debauched, that person possesses a condition of health or a state of debauchery. A state that someone possesses, then, is always a state *of* something (e.g., of temperance or cowardice); a condition someone possesses is always a condition *of* something (e.g., of health or illness); knowledge is always knowledge *of* something (for example, grammar or geometry). These linguistic cues in the Greek help flag the relatives. Usually, relatives are signaled by the genitive case when the genitive has the force of "of" or "than." They are also signaled by the dative case when the dative has the force of "to," as when we say that "*x* is similar *to* something else" (*Categories* 6b9). And relatives sometimes are signaled by *pros* followed by the correlative in the accusative case, as in the case of "is relative to another" (*Categories* 6b8, 6a37).

So far the text indicates at least the following kinds of genitives as linguistic markers for relational being: genitives of measure, e.g., following "double" *(diplasion),* e.g., with genitives of comparison, such as "larger" *(meizon),* and genitives of quality, e.g., the genitive for what a state *(hexis)* is a state of. Later, Aristotle finds that *L* allows for certain partitive genitives—the genitives that reflect a thing's being a part of something (e.g., a hand being part of a body). As we will discover, however, these partitive genitives become problematic and cause Aristotle to question whether, say, someone's head or hand really ought to be considered a relative.

According to *Topics* 124b35–125a13 we can identify relative expressions by the grammatical inflections they take. For example, relatives are sometimes expressed as "to something" *(tini)* or "of something" *(tinos),* which take the dative and genitive cases, respectively. Cavarnos notes a similar explanation in the *Politics* (Cavarnos 1975, 44). Speaking on justice and equality, Aristotle reports people say that "what is just is just *for* someone" (*Politics* 1282b20–21). In addition, Aristotle's definition of anger states that anger "must always be felt *toward* some particular individual" (*Rhetoric* 1378a31 ff., trans. Rhys Roberts; italics mine. See also *Rhetoric* 1382a5).

Ackrill has several concerns with Aristotle's use of *L* (Ackrill 1963, 99). One worry is that the *L* criterion sets the threshold for relational being so low that simply meeting certain grammatical conditions permits a thing to be *L*-compliant and therefore, genuinely relative. But since this admits unworthy interlopers into the category, Ackrill believes that *L* cannot be the proper criterion to secure the category for genuine relatives.

Aristotle is well aware of the pitfalls of relying too heavily on grammatical or linguistic criteria to delimit the category and directly takes up the issue in the chapter on opposites at *Categories* 10. There he states that things may be opposed to each other in four ways: as relatives, as contraries, as privation (or possession), and as affirmation (or negation) (*Categories* 11b17). Restating *L* nearly verbatim, Aristotle explains that when things are opposed as relatives, they are opposed to each other by being "just what they are *of* their opposites or in some other way in relation to one another" (*Categories* 11b33). But when they are opposed as contraries, they are not relatives. Aristotle goes on to say, in effect, that just because contraries meet *L*'s linguistic criterion of being called "of" one another, contraries are not "just what they are" *of* one another. For instance, Aristotle states that good and bad are contraries of each other. But simply because they are contraries *of* each other, we should not assume that they belong to the category of relation. "Good" is not just what it is *of* its opposite: Good is not called *good* of the bad (*Categories* 11b35). Rather, good is called the *contrary of* the bad (*Categories* 11b34–6).

This does not mean Aristotle is averse to relying on grammatical aids in his consideration of the category of relation. Far from it. What we have seen so far of Aristotle's first account of relational being attests to this. Elsewhere (*Topics* IV.4), Aristotle encourages the dialectician to consider, when the things stated bear a relation to each other, whether the genus is inflected in the same manner that the species is:

> For as the species is used, so should the genus be as well, as in the case of double and its higher genera; for both double and multiple are *of-something (tinos)*. Likewise, also, in the case of knowledge; for both knowledge itself and its genera, e.g., disposition and state, are *of-something (tinos)*. (*Topics* 124b36–125a1)[14]

Nevertheless, despite *L*'s utility in providing this first pass at a criterion for the category, in the end, Aristotle recognizes that *L* allows too much into the category of relation. Eventually, Aristotle finds *L* inadequate because it does not exclude from the category those things that truly are not relatives. Consequently, *L* fails to capture what makes a thing genuinely relative (*Categories* 8a31–35).

Ackrill also contends that it is not clear why Aristotle calls state and condition relatives as when Aristotle says that each of these "is called what it is (and not something else) *of* other things" (*Categories* 6b3–4). Ackrill suggests Aristotle may think such words as 'state' and 'condition' are always followed by a word that takes the genitive and that further specifies the word, as is the case with 'state': A state must be a state of a specific kind (Ackrill 1963, 99). If any word similarly could be specified further, it would likewise be considered a relative. Ackrill asserts that if this is what Aristotle intends, Aristotle "will be committed to counting as relatives a vast number of terms which he in fact puts into other categories."

Ackrill's alarm is unfounded. Not only will Aristotle ultimately close the linguistic loopholes that allow nearly anything to be a relative, but, as already indicated, Aristotle is perfectly aware that we ought to use linguistic analysis judiciously when relegating items to their categories and delimiting the categories themselves. Perhaps, in Ackrill's translation of the *Categories*, where he uses "state" and "condition" he would have done better to use "possession" and "disposition" for *hexis* and *diathesis* or to stick with the old Oxford translations: "habit" and "disposition" (Edghill 1928, 18). These latter words would then fit the prepositional requirement of taking "of" or "toward" to introduce their correlative objects. Had Ackrill used "possession" and "disposition" in his translation, the objects they intend might have been more evident to him: A science or a virtue is a *possession* of a field of objects, i.e., things to be known or right things to be done.

At *Categories* 6b6–11, Aristotle restates *L* and offers a third set of examples that expand on the first set:

> Relatives, then, are called just what they are *of* other things or in some manner *toward* another thing. For example, a mountain is called <u>large</u> relative to another thing (for a mountain is called 'large' in relation to something), and the similar is called 'similar' to something, and others such as these are likewise said to be in relation to something.

This third set of examples provides a good opportunity to see why it is difficult to say exactly what Aristotle takes a relative to be.

Categories 6b8–9 says that:

> A mountain is called <u>large</u> relative to another thing (for a mountain is called 'large' in relation to something).

And later at *Categories* 6b8–11:

> A mountain is called <u>large</u> relative to another thing (for a mountain is called 'large' in relation to something), and the similar is called 'similar' to something, and others such as these are likewise said to be in relation to something.

What exactly is the relative here? Is it the concrete item, i.e., the mountain? Is it the adjectival word 'large'? Is it the metaphysical predicate <u>large</u> or <u>larger</u>? Is it perhaps the instance of the attribute <u>being</u> <u>large</u> that inheres in the mountain?

As I will discuss at length below in Part Two, commentators agree that Aristotle considers a relative to be something indicative of a relatedness of one thing to another, but a wide range of opinion exists about what these things are that are in relationship to each other. As we work through Aristotle's account of relatives in the *Categories*, I believe it will become apparent that at various points in the text Aristotle has a range of relational entity in mind when he speaks about relatives. What we can do now, though, is affirm Aristotle's basic intuition about relatives (however they ultimately are construed): Being a relative means being related to or being in relationship with another thing. Aristotle's two examples concerning largeness suggest two analyses of what it means—at this juncture at least—for a thing to be a relational entity. The first (*Categories* 6a38) is a straightforward case of a comparative relationship: One thing, x, is being compared to another thing, y. When we compare a mountain to something else, such as a house or a car, the mountain comes out ahead as larger than either of those items. The second (*Categories* 6b8–9) tells us that a mountain's being called 'large' must involve something other than the mountain itself. *L* confirms this analysis because it says that for a thing to be a relative, that thing must be in relation *to* something. Although we can interpret this example as we did the example at *Categories* 6a38, textual evidence from Aristotle's discussion of quantity in *Categories* 6 suggests that he may have another kind of comparative relationship in mind as well.

At *Categories* 5b16–22, for instance, Aristotle explains why certain items are relatives, not quantities:

> For nothing is called <u>large</u> or <u>small</u> just in itself, but by reference to something else. For example, a mountain is called 'small' yet a grain of millet 'large'—because one is larger than the other things of its kind while the other is smaller than other things of its kind. (trans. Ackrill)

What Aristotle means is that when we consider mountains and grains of millet large or small, we consider them to be this way with respect to other items in their respective classes. Aristotle reiterates this point in the next example he offers when he explains why few and many are not quantities but relatives instead.

Again, we say that there are many people in the village but few in Athens—although there are many times more people [in Athens] than [in the village]. (*Categories* 5b22–25)

Whatever is few or many is so in relation to something else. In this case, the "something else" is the number of persons that a village has as far as villages go and the population in a thriving city as far as populations of thriving cities go. In both cases, the things Aristotle calls relatives are so because of a sortal comparison that contextually relates one item with other members of its class. What the examples at *Categories* 5b16–25, 6a38, and 6b8–9 reveal, then, is Aristotle's sense that being relational requires the involvement of two items, whether they be discreet individuals, classes, or an individual and some class of individuals.

Aristotle expands on his earlier comments at *Categories* 6b2 ff and presents a fourth set of examples of relatives :

Lying, standing, and sitting are certain positions, and position is a relative. To-be-lying, to-be-standing, or to-be-sitting are not themselves positions, but are named paronymously from the positions just mentioned. (*Categories* 6b11–14).

Here the words 'lying' and 'standing' are nouns and refer to a certain posture or particular position of a thing. The second series of expressions ('to-be-lying', 'to-be-standing', and so forth) are infinitives with articles, or what are called articular infinitives. Articular infinitives are grammatical nouns, but they retain some of the features of verbs in that they can take objects or be modified by adverbs.

Aristotle includes position in the category of relation, but it is not clear whether he means to include the different positions there are (e.g., lying, standing) as relatives. Morales states that Aristotle uses the relational genus of position as a means of defining the species of positions under it, so that lying is defined as "the position of an animal that rests horizontally" (Morales 1994, 270). According to *Metaphysics* 1021b3–6, it would appear that Aristotle does take lying and standing to be positions. Some things are included in the category of relation, Aristotle says, because their genus happens to be a relation. There, medicine is thought to be a relative because knowledge, its genus, is thought to be a relative. The same reasoning could be applied here: The genus of lying or standing is position, and position is a relative.

On the other hand, if Aristotle wants to exclude the species of position from the category of relation, perhaps it is because they fail to meet the linguistic standards L prescribes—namely, that of being called "of" or "than" another thing. What is called "lying" is not called "lying" *of* or *than* something. Nor is "lying" in "some other way" *relative* to something (see *Categories* 6a36–37). Neither does Aristotle count being in a position (e.g., "is lying," "is standing") as relative, as he considers "is lying" and the like paronymously named or derived from the particular positions (*Categories* 11b10).

2.2 The Marks of Relatives

After presenting the first account of relational being and offering some examples, Aristotle discusses six features, or marks, of relatives. I briefly restate these features in my own words, designating the marks "M1," "M2," and so on. The first mark of relatives (M1) is given at *Categories* 6b15:

> M1   Some, but not all, relatives have contraries.

Knowledge, for example, is contrary to ignorance, but that which is double has no contrary. The same is true of numbers. The number 4 is the double of 2, but the number 4 has no contrary. The second mark of relatives appears at *Categories* 6b19:

> M2   Some relatives admit of degrees.

Some relatives admit of a more and a less. For instance, although Butterfly is less similar to Mimi than she is to Dido, one cannot say that the number 4 is more the double of the number 2 than 8 is the double of 4.

Aristotle gives the third mark at *Categories* 6b28:

> M3   Every relative item has another relative item, its
> correlative, with which it is associated reciprocally.

Aristotle devotes nearly a third of *Categories* 7 to examining M3. M3 consists of two important claims. First, all relatives have correlatives. Second, all relatives form reciprocal relationships with their correlatives. Both of these features again provide evidence that Aristotle conceives of relational being as always requiring at least two paired items. We have seen that, for Aristotle, relatives are always conceived of with respect to some other thing. Here he specifies that a relative always has its relational "partner," or correlative. The two form a relational pair: the entity that refers (i.e., the referent or relative) and that to which the referent refers (i.e., the referendum or correlative). Aristotle gives master-slave, double-half, and larger-smaller as examples of relative-correlative pairs (*Categories* 6b28–31; see also *Categories* 6a37, *Topics* 142a28–31, and *Sophistical Refutations* 181b25–28).

Aristotle now insists that relatives reciprocate each other (6b36 ff.). Stating that every relative has its reciprocal is another way for Aristotle to say that every relative has its converse. In the *Categories*, Aristotle's position is that relatives are reciprocal and convertible irrespective of the symmetry or asymmetry of the relations connected with them. At *Metaphysics* V.15 1021a29–1021b3, however, Aristotle will drop the reciprocity requirement. There he distinguishes one group of relatives— the measurable, the knowable, and the thinkable—by the fact that they do not exhibit reciprocity.

But no haphazard pairing of things will do; relatives must form appropriately articulated, reciprocal pairs.

> All relatives, then, if indeed they are given properly, are spoken of in relation to correlatives that reciprocate. Since, indeed, if it is given in relation to a chance thing and not in relation to that which it is spoken of, it does not reciprocate. I mean that even the relatives that are said to be reciprocal and that have established names, none of these reciprocates if the relative is given of accidental things and is not given in relation to which it is spoken. (*Categories* 7a22–30)

We see, then, that relatives and their correlatives must be given properly to pinpoint exactly how they reciprocate. (See also *Topics* 149b4–23, where Aristotle discusses the importance of stating exactly the object to which a relative is related, and *Posterior Analytics* 73b25–74a3, where he stresses the importance of noting what pertains primarily and not by chance when we state what holds of something universally.) In addition to saying that all relatives must have reciprocating correlatives, Aristotle further notes that we can take advantage of linguistic phenomena to make the relational words reciprocate each other. In fact, at *Categories* 7a5–7 Aristotle insists that we invent words, if necessary, to ensure the reciprocity between the two relational items.

Aristotle gives some examples. What is the correlative item to a wing? Since other things besides birds have wings (e.g., bats and mosquitoes), the proper reciprocal correlative to "wing" is not "bird."

According to Aristotle "it is not as being a bird that a wing is said to be of it (*Categories* 6b38–39, trans. Ackrill).

Rather, the correct reciprocating correlative would be a "winged" thing. Aristotle concludes, although rather elliptically:

> Thus, if it is given properly, it reciprocates, e.g., a wing is a wing of a winged thing and a winged thing is a thing winged with a wing. (*Categories* 7a3–5)

Differences in ending (e.g., '-able' and '-ible') and differences in translating the grammatical particles involved with relative words also facilitate adapting language to meet the demands of the expression relational reciprocity. Aristotle illustrates this with the relative words 'knowledge' and 'perception'. Aristotle understands that on their own, the words 'knowledge' and 'knowable' are not properly reciprocating (or convertible) expressions. Although it makes sense to say "Knowledge is of what is knowable," its reciprocal statement, "What is knowable is of knowledge," does not make sense. We can, however, make the words 'knowable' and 'knowledge' reciprocal:

> For example, knowledge is called knowledge of what is knowable and what is knowable is knowable by knowledge, and of perception, perception is perception of a perceptible thing and the perceptible is perceptible by perception. (*Categories* 6b33–36)

As Kirwan (1971, 165) notes, it is just the situation here in which one says that "the perceptible is perceptible *by* perception" that offers an example of what Aristotle has in mind when he speaks of things being relative in "some other way"—i.e., other than their being expressed as *of* or *than* other items (*Categories* 6b37). In this case, the relational nature of the item is expressed through its being *by*, not *of* or *than*, another item. The words are made reciprocal (and convertible) by rendering each word's ending differently—adding the Greek suffix '-*ton*'. As Smyth notes, adjectival verbal nouns with the '-*ton*' suffix, such as 'perceptible' *(aisthēton)* and 'knowable' *(epistēton)*, can have the force of a perfect passive participle, as in "the perceived" or "that which has been perceived". But these adjectival verbal nouns also may carry the force of possibility, as in "the perceivable" or "that which is able to be perceived" (see Smyth 1983, 107, 358.2.b.). This leads to ambiguity for it is not always clear whether the verbal adjective ought to be rendered as referring to something that is past as opposed to something that presently possible.

In any event, addition of the suffix to the words 'knowledge' and 'perception' allows Aristotle to demonstrate the reciprocal relationship between the words. Although almost any word can be refashioned in this manner, it is not Aristotle's intention to treat language as a plaything. He remarks that the above procedure of coining words offers the "easiest way to grasp things for which names are not established" (*Categories* 7a18–19).

Aristotle is serious about requiring the correlativity of the relative-correlative pairs, as his example at *Categories* 7a31–7b9 shows. He carefully excludes substance as not directly relevant to the importance of maintaining the correlativity between relational items. What is the correlative to a slave? Simply being a human being is not enough to count as the correlative item for a slave because 'human being' does not identify or isolate that *particular* thing of which the slave is called. A slave is not a slave of a biped or even slave of a rational animal; rather, a slave can only be a slave of a master. In this example, Aristotle abstracts what ordinarily is most fundamental in his meta-ontology—substance (i.e., a human being)—and retains what is accidental to substance—being a master—all in the name of securing the relationship between relative and correlative.

Aristotle's discussion of M3 makes clear that he understands that certain characteristics go hand in hand with what it means to be a relative entity. Namely, besides affirming the general "towardness" that is characteristic of relational being, he conceives of relatives as pairs of items. That is, he maintains that relatives stand in a two-termed, or dyadic, relationship as relative and correlative. Moreover, his comments on the exact reciprocity relatives must have certainly suggest that he would consider the pair of relative items "ordered" insofar as the relative-correlative pair have to be given properly or stipulated so that the dyadic nature of the relation between the two items is maintained.

Aristotle continues with the fourth mark of relational entities:

M4   Most relatives exist simultaneously with their correlatives.
       (*Categories* 7b15)

It may seem odd at first for Aristotle to give M4 as a mark for relatives. Indeed, more than any other non-substantial accident, relatives have to be ontologically simultaneous with their underlying ontological foundation. But by including M4 Aristotle makes an important point.

M4 indicates that the simultaneity of relatives cannot be the dependence the accident "white" has with its subject substance. Why?

First, if Aristotle is characterizing the general relationship between substance and accident, he makes a serious error in stating that only "most" of a certain species of accident is simultaneous—i.e., simultaneous in the sense of being dependent—upon its subject. *Categories* 2a34-35 says that no accident exists without substance. Since every accident is dependent upon its foundation, the only point Aristotle can be making with M4 is that besides the dependency relationship characteristic of substance and all the predicaments, another distinctively relational connection exists between relatives and their correlatives. What Aristotle believes is most significant here is not the relational entity's relationship to its *subject*, but its relationship to its *correlative*. The correlativity of the two items, and here in the *Categories* at least, their reciprocity, is what determines the character of the simultaneity that most relatives have.

In addition to stressing the point that most relatives must exist simultaneously, Aristotle makes it clear that two items are necessary whenever we have an actual (i.e., concrete) relative. That which is double and that which is half must exist simultaneously in order for either thing to exist as a relative or correlative, otherwise "they would destroy one another," Aristotle says, "for when there is not a double, there is not a half" (*Categories* 7b19–21).

He observes, however, that the simultaneity of relatives holds only for the most part. In a rather long section (*Categories* 7b15–8a12), Aristotle contends that the relationship between relatives is produced, sustained, or severed depending on the simultaneity, priority, or posteriority of the entities involved. For instance, the lack of simultaneity leads to an asymmetrical relationship between some relatives.

> For the knowable would seem to be prior to knowledge. For the most part, it is of things already existing that we acquire knowledge. For in few cases, if any, could one find knowledge coming into being simultaneously with what is knowable. (*Categories* 7b24–27)

So, unlike converse relations such as <u>is a slave of</u> and <u>is a master of</u> or symmetrical relations such as <u>is equal to</u> whose terms must be existentially simultaneous, it is unusual to have knowledge or perception of something without the object of that knowledge or perception existing before it has been encountered by us. One possible exception might be that of a musician and an improvisation she creates. If she is at the piano improvising, her perception of the improvisation and the perceptible (i.e., the music itself) come into being simultaneously. Her perception of the music occurs at the same time as its existence as a perceptible.

Aristotle further describes the existential asymmetry between certain relatives by stating that:

> when the knowable is destroyed, it destroys knowledge also with it, but knowledge does not take the knowable to destruction. For if there is not a knowable, there is not knowledge since there will no longer be knowledge of anything, but if there is not knowledge of something, there is nothing to hinder the existence of a knowable. (*Categories* 7b27–31)

Here I take it that Aristotle is not using his strong sense of scientific knowledge, i.e., *epistēmē*. Rather, Aristotle's point is that my knowledge of a known thing, say, Billy Strayhorn's "Lush Life," depends on the song's prior existence. But the contrary is not true: "Lush Life" remains a knowable object of knowledge even if I have never heard of the song at all. The song remains a *possible* object of knowledge whether I know of the song or not (*Categories* 7b27–33).

Next, Aristotle says that "[i]f animal is destroyed, there is not knowledge, but there may be many knowables" (*Categories* 7b33–35). What Aristotle means is that whether I, as an animal, exist or not, sculptures, songs, and many other things will remain to be knowables for others. At *De Anima* 417b22–24, he contrasts what knowledge and sensation apprehend. Knowledge, Aristotle says, apprehends universals, which are "in a sense within the soul itself," and this explains why persons can think anytime they want to. What sensation apprehends, on the other hand, are sensible individuals (e.g., a particular color or flavor) that are external to us and do not depend on us as animals in order to be sensibles. They only depend on us to be sensed. It is this latter case that Aristotle highlights at *Categories* 7b35 ff.

Aristotle continues with another example of the asymmetry between some relatives. He says that:

> the perceptible seems to be prior to perception since the perceptible, being destroyed, destroys perception along with it, but perception does not carry the perceptible to destruction. For perception is concerned with body and in body, and if the perceptible is destroyed, body too is destroyed, since body is also a perceptible; and if there is not body, perception is also destroyed. So, the perceptible carries perception to

destruction. However, perception does not destroy the perceptible. (*Categories* 7b36–8a4)

Aristotle's point is that the perceptible still exists even without a perceiver, i.e., without perception occurring. If my mother, Lois, is dressing a wound on one of her patients and momentarily blinks her eyes, the perceptible (the wound) still exists even though her perception of the wound ceases. Blinking her eyes does not destroy the wound. But if there were no wound, then perception would be "destroyed" as there would be nothing (i.e., no wound) to perceive.

For the most part Aristotle's view is that perceptible objects exist independently and prior to perception, not that perception brings the perceptible into existence. The exception to this account of the asymmetrical nature of perception occurs when he considers the perceptible as actualized in conjunction with an actual act of perception. Aristotle then takes the position that, strictly speaking, the actually perceived object and the actual perception of it come into being simultaneously.

2.3 The *aporia* Regarding Substance

What we know thus far is that something is a relative if it complies with *L* and meets M1-M4. Aristotle contends that every relative has not just its correlative but a reciprocating correlative, even if words for the latter must be custom made for the occasion. This reciprocity demand illustrates Aristotle's insistence on treating relatives—conceptually, linguistically, and concretely—as two items that must stand in relation to each other as the dyad, i.e., the two terms, in a relation would.

We have also seen Aristotle's preoccupation with language as he explores the ways in which we think about, or conceive of, relational entities. Indeed, as already noted, given *L*, it looks as though anything that satisfies the linguistic criterion of being called or said *of* something else (i.e., anything expressible in conjunction with a particular partitive or possessive genitive) counts as a relative. This means that merely being called *of* something else—say, the cow *of* Mrs. O'Leary or the hand *of* a person—is enough to qualify that thing as a relational entity.

This situation leads Aristotle to grapple with an *aporia* (or problem): Can we exclude substance from the category of relation?

> It is a problem *(aporia)* whether, as seems to be the case, no substance is said to be a relative or whether this is possible with regard to some secondary substances. (*Categories* 8a13)

Aristotle quickly finds ontological as well as grammatical reasons to exclude the wholes or parts of primary substances, and most secondary substances, from the category of relation. He says:

> In the case of primary substance, it is true (that they are not relatives) for neither wholes nor parts are said in relation to something *(pros ti legetai)*. For the individual man is not called *(legetai)* "someone's individual man," nor is an individual cow called "someone's individual cow." (*Categories* 8a15–19)

Given his earlier treatment of substance (*Categories* 5), it is not surprising that Aristotle excludes primary substance from the category. The ontological independence of primary substance means that primary substance is not conceived of with respect to some other thing, and this failure precludes primary substance from being *L*-compliant.

Now it may be objected that primary substance is indeed conceived of with respect to its constituent elements: matter and form. A primary substance would not exist, after all, if it were not for some matter being individuated by some form. But with Aristotle's treatment of the *aporia*, he seems to have in mind an already individuated item, an item that does not depend on another entity in order to be what it is. A goldfish is an individuated substance, i.e., a primary substance, and there is no other entity the goldfish needs to be related to in order for it to exist as a goldfish. This is not the case with a slave or a master because each must be related to the other in order for it to be what it is.

These same reasons provide a linguistic rationale for excluding primary substance from the category of relation. No primary substance word is expressed grammatically with respect to another thing. Consider, for instance, Bessie the cow *(bous)*. Bessie is an individual cow and hence is a primary substance. From Aristotle's perspective it would be ungrammatical to say that she is someone's *individual* cow *(tinos tis bous)*, for example, Mrs. O'Leary's *individual* cow. What makes the locution ungrammatical is the presence of the indefinite pronoun for "something" or "some one" *(tis)*. The pronoun '*tis*' is often used to exploit a Greek linguistic convention for calling attention to the particularity of a discrete item. The same ontological and grammatical grounds also provide a reason to exclude the parts of primary substances and most secondary substances from the category of relation. Aristotle says that an individual head is not called "someone's *individual* head" but is called "someone's head" (*Categories* 8a20–21). And concerning secondary substance, he asserts that just as one would not call an individual man "someone's *individual* man" (*Categories*

8a16–17), neither would one call a man "someone's man":

> For example, a man is not called "someone's man" nor a cow "someone's cow" nor a log "someone's log," but it is called "someone's property." (*Categories* 8a22–24)

The distinction Aristotle makes here is between a specimen from the species and the species itself: Tucker may own Peggy, a specimen of the species *Homo sapiens*, but he does not own the species itself.

However, Aristotle says that some secondary substances remain problematic (*Categories* 8a24–26). For example, a head is called someone's head, and a hand is called someone's hand (*Categories* 8a26–28). There are two reasons why these substances appear to be relatives. First, they meet the "genitive-friendly" linguistic requirements of *L:* Uttering the phrase "someone's head" is linguistically equivalent to uttering the phrase "the head *of* someone." And second, they meet *L*'s requirement of being conceived of *(legetai)* something. Having a (human) head is something we conceive of with respect to being human, and so head remains *L*-compliant. It is the fact that a head is indeed called and conceived of as "someone's head" that makes it, and substances like it, still seem *L*-compliant.

2.4 Aristotle's Second Account of Relatives

Are heads and hands really the kind of thing Aristotle wants to include as categorical relational entities? Absolutely not. Both are parts of substances, and neither of them can be, as to their whole being, purely relative. Yet, Aristotle says, as long as *L* is the only operative criterion it is "exceedingly difficult or impossible to show that no substance is a relative." (*Categories* 8a29–31)

Weinberg (1965, 72) comments that "[f]or reasons not wholly clear" Aristotle proposes a second definition. On the contrary, I think the reason is crystal clear: Aristotle knows that the mere fact that one thing, *A*, is conceived of with reference to another thing, *B*, does not make *A* fundamentally relative. Aristotle plainly needs a more restrictive account to represent the distinctive kind of being that the category of relation demands. This revised account of relational being appears at *Categories* 8a31–35:

> But if it [i.e., the former formulation] was inadequate and if those things are relative for which being is the same as holding in some way toward something (*esti ta pros ti hois to einai tauton esti tō pros ti pōs*

echein), then perhaps some answer may be found [i.e., some way of excluding substance from the category]. The previous definition holds good for all relatives, but indeed this—their being called *of* other things—is not the same as what their being relatives is.

I call this second formulation "*E*"—I use the letter '*E*' to emphasize the importance of the word *einai* in the second formation— and call relatives that meet *E*, "*E* relatives," "*E* entities," or I will say that they are "*E*-compliant," and so forth. I have translated *E* quite literally in order to highlight its two components. The first component is the "being" *(to einai)* construction, which replaces the "is called", "is conceived of" *(legetai)* construction of *L*. My designations are somewhat in keeping, then, with the scholastic distinction between *legetai* or *einai* relatives. *L* relatives will become labeled "*relationes secundum dici*" (relatives with respect to how they are said or expressed) and *E* relatives labeled "*relationes secundum esse*" (relatives with respect to their being or existence) (see, e.g., Ackrill 1963, 101 and Thomas Aquinas, *Summa Theologiae* I, q. 13, a. 7, ad 1). The second component of *E* is the "holding in some way toward" *(pros ti pōs echein)* construction, or simply the "holding somehow" construction.

2.5 The Being Component

Aristotle intends *E* to provide a way to distinguish between entities that belong in the category of relation (i.e., categorical relatives) and those that do not. *E* says that things are relative "for which being is the same as holding in some way toward something" (*Categories* 8a32). In order to understand how this standard applies to categorical relatives and not to non-categorical relatives, we must first distinguish two senses of "being"—I will call them "existential" and "essential"—and then ask which is at play here.

Suppose Aristotle is using "being" in its existential sense of "to exist as an actual concrete item," i.e., "to exist objectually." We know that Aristotle considers concrete items (i.e., primary substances) the "most real" entities, and so concrete relational items appear to be natural candidates for genuine relatives. Now if *E* relatives are concrete existent items and if existing for them is the same as holding somehow toward something, then it looks as though authentic relatives must exist simultaneously: Actual slaves with actual masters would count as *E* relatives.

A problem exists, however, with adopting an existential interpretation of *E* as just sketched out. If what Aristotle is saying is that the being of a relative is fundamentally about the relative's concrete existence, *E* will still leave Aristotle with the task of delineating what is relational, *per se*, about relational being. Even if we make it clear that actual concrete relatives are substances that possess relational properties and are not just concrete items, what remains missing from an existential reading of *E* is an account of relational being that deals solely with what allows these relational entities to be relational in the first place.

Rather than adopting an exclusively existential reading of the "being" (*to einai*) construction, we also should look to incorporate an essential reading as well. What Aristotle is after, I believe, is a formula that typifies relational being but in a way that attempts to provide a basis for what it means to be *completely* relational, and to do this he needs *E* to isolate features that are genuinely emblematic of the category of relation alone. The components of *E*, therefore, should convey the idea that a relative's reason for being relative lies *only* in its being related to something else, i.e., in its "relationality", if you will. An essential reading of the being construction can do this because it helps characterize what is representative of relational being when no immediate consideration is given to concrete items. If I am right, then the central focus *E* is on relational metaphysical predicates or universals, and not so much on concrete relational items.

Nevertheless, if Aristotle has the task of prescribing the essential features of the category of relation, he still has the task of showing what makes possible the true predication of items that do have relational attributes. To accomplish this task, he must be just as concerned about how relatives behave in actual, existential cases as he is with delimiting the essential and metaphysical boundaries of the category of relation. Later on (*Categories* 8b6 ff.) Aristotle tests the *E* account of relatives against actual cases of relatives. This indicates that existential issues are ultimately as important to him as are essential and metaphysical ones when confirming whether something belongs to the category of relation or not.

Aristotle does not explicitly spell out how these existential and metaphysical requirements should work together. It is likely he is silent on the issue because he takes the ontological, and consequently, the existential dependence of attributes on their subjects to be a non-controversial element of his ontology and something he has already elaborated on sufficiently, for example, at *Categories* 1a20 ff.

2.6 The Holding Somehow Component

The holding somehow component is anchored around the adverb "somehow" *(pōs)* and the verb "to hold" or "to have" *(echein)*. This holding somehow *(tō pros ti pōs echein)* construction expresses more than just the fact that to be relative means being related to something. In effect, the construction isolates something that in modern logic would be akin to a logical relational predicate or relational function in the sentence '*x* is R of *y*' (or '*x*R*y*') where 'R' stands for any *E*-compliant relational attribute. To see how this interpretation is possible, we must begin by analyzing the constituent elements of the holding somehow construction.

There are four elements to consider: (i) the relative; (ii) a "holding somehow"; (iii) toward; and (iv) the something, i.e., the correlative entity. As we have seen thus far in *Categories* 7, Aristotle has thoroughly discussed features of elements (i), (iii), and (iv). He has discussed relatives at length and given examples of them, element (i); he has described the general "towardsness" of relatives whether this relationality is expressed as a thing's being *of*, *than*, *to*, or in some other way conceived of in relation to some other thing, element (iii); and he has commented at length about the necessary correlativity of relatives, element (iv).

Element (ii), the holding somehow component, acts to differentiate the uninstantiated relational predicate from all other features of relational being, i.e., from elements (i), (iii), and (iv). The holding somehow component acts as what I shall call the "relation indicator" in *E*, specifying that being genuinely relational entails a "holding somehow", element (ii), of one thing, element (i), toward, element (iii), another thing, element (iv). What the holding somehow component shows is what I believe on Aristotle's view is the incompleteness or "gappiness" of relationality. The holding somehow component must be supplemented or completed by mention of the relative and its correlative as is illustrated by an analysis of the *E* relative <u>slave</u>. The relative <u>slave</u> involves the particular kind of relationality of being a human being owned by a human being—i.e., a holding somehow—of one thing (Peggy) toward another thing (Tucker).

2.7 Is *L* Still Necessary?

If *E* does such a good job of disclosing the fundamental character of relation, should Aristotle abandon *L*? Is *L* of no further use? The *L* formulation might seem to indicate a marker for exclusively non-categorical relations, but it does not. In order to have a non-categorical relation in this context, it would be necessary to understand an "only" with the "said toward" *(legetai pros)* formula, *L*, and we have none. All relatives, categorical and non-categorical alike, are conceived of with reference to other appropriate items. But the categorical relative (e.g., slave) is an entirely relative reality. That is all it is. On the other hand, the non-categorical relative (e.g., state) is not only a relative, but is also an entity in some other category. The hope, then, is that *E* will provide a way to exclude substance from the category while admitting that some of the entities may be relatives in the broader, non-categorical sense of satisfying *L*.

According to *Categories* 8a33–35, *E* does not rescind *L;* it augments it:

> The previous definition (*L*) holds good for all relatives, but indeed this—their being called *of* other things—is not the same as what their being relatives is.

What this means is that the new, more accurate understanding of what it means to be relational will include what *L* does well: enable Aristotle to show that a relative is said with respect to something else, and yet go beyond this. *L*'s continued inclusion as a criterion, therefore, is important.

Based on our findings so far, we can say at least three things about what it takes for a relative to be *E*-compliant: First, it must be *L*-compliant; second, it must have the characteristic of being wholly and completely relational; and third, it must in some way require specification of the items with which the relationship is formed or sustained.

Furthermore, we know that every *E* relative also meets the linguistic standards of *L;* but it is clear that not every *L*-relative entity meets the standards for being an *E* entity. For example, slave meets both *E* and *L:* Being a slave means being in a particular relationship with another individual. We can also render the word 'slave' appropriately. But take, for instance, the word 'pen' in the proposition "the *pen* of Pamela". 'Pen' meets *L* because it can be expressed as a possessive genitive. However, a thing's being *L*-compliant no longer guarantees that the item is a true relative. Being for a fountain pen is not the same as its being related somehow to some other thing. No "holding somehow" component is at play with respect to either the essential or existential being of a fountain pen. To be a fountain pen is to be an instrument for writing and therefore to have certain properties (e.g., having a nib, being able to contain and to release ink, and so forth). It is an *accident* of a pen's existence that is owned by someone. But this is not the case with a slave because being a slave requires the slave to be owned by someone. On the basis of *E*, then, we can exclude not only an artifact, the fountain pen in my hand, but more importantly primary substances such as Bessie the cow, from the category of relation.

2.8 The Fifth Mark of Relatives: *Categories* 8a35–8b14

Aristotle thinks that the problem about including substance in the category of relation is resolved by what follows from *E*.

> From the above [i.e., the second formulation of relational being] it is clear that if someone knows definitely that a thing is one of the relatives he will also know definitely that in relation to which it is spoken of. This is evident even on the face of it. For if someone knows of a certain thing (*tis tode ti*) that it is one of the relatives, and being for [relatives] is the same thing as holding somehow in relation to a thing, he also knows that toward which it is holding somehow. For if he does not know at all that towards which it is holding somehow, neither will he know if it is holding somehow towards something. And regarding particular cases (*tôn kath' hekasta*) this sort of thing is clear. For example, if a person knows definitely of a 'this' that it is double, he knows definitely at once of what it is double. For if a person by no means knows it to be double of something definite, neither will he know at all whether it is double. And similarly, if he also knows that a 'this' is more beautiful, it is also necessary that he know, because of this, what thing it is more beautiful than. (He will not know in an indefinite way that this thing is more beautiful than an inferior thing). (*Categories* 8a36–8b9)

Let us take up the parts of the passage one at a time.

> From the above [i.e., the second formulation of relational being] it is clear that (1) if someone knows definitely that a thing is one of the relatives (2) he will also know definitely that in relation to which it is spoken of. (3) This is evident even on the face of it. (*Categories* 8a36–38)

What so clearly follows from *E*, Aristotle says, is the following:

(4) For if someone knows of a certain thing (*tis tode ti*) that it is one of the relatives, and (5) being for [relatives] is the same thing as holding somehow in relation to a thing, (6) he also knows that toward which it is holding somehow. (7) For if he does not know at all that towards which it is holding somehow, (8) neither will he know if it is holding somehow towards something. (*Categories* 8a38–8b3)

We have seen that Aristotle thinks being relational means having a "holding somehow" relationship with some other thing. Now he claims that whatever is genuinely relational, i.e., whatever meets E such that it has a holding somehow relationship with some other thing, must also comply with a strict epistemic standard: When a relative is known definitely, that towards which it is holding somehow must be known definitely, too. This gives us the fifth mark of relatives:

[M5] Knowing definitely that something is a relative entails knowing definitely that towards which it is holding somehow. (*Categories* 8a36–7)

According to M5, if you know definitely that a thing is one of the relatives, then you will also be in a position to know definitely that towards which the thing stands in relation, i.e., the relative's correlative. All genuine relatives, therefore, must meet an exacting epistemological requirement. Let us call this the "knowing definitely criterion":

The knowing definitely criterion

If a certain thing definitely is known to be a relative, then its correlative must also be known definitely. (*Categories* 8a36–8b3)[15]

The Ambiguity of tode ti

Even though Aristotle presents the knowing definitely criterion in a straightforward manner, the criterion and its relationship to E are not without interpretive difficulties. First of all, the text is open to different interpretations in one key spot. The ambiguous text appears at *Categories* 8a38 where Aristotle writes "*tis tode ti*"—three Greek words that combine two separate expressions: '*tis*' and '*tode ti*'. There are three points of possible ambiguity. The first involves the translation of *tode ti*. Now *tode ti* typically is translated to indicate either (a) the non-specific or general mention of a thing or (b) the general mention of a thing and its genus or kind. For instance, one literal translation of (a) would be "a this" or "a thing" where *tode ti* is put to the same sort of use as the phrase "a man" would be where what is being referred to is any member of the class of *Homo sapiens*, not the species *Homo sapiens*, nor any special, particular member of the species.

In the case of (b), *tode ti* might be translated literally as "a this something". Here two things are signified. The first thing signified is "*a this*", i.e., something that can be pointed out demonstratively. Here, an item is indicated, but its mention is still general. Second, a kind of thing or a class of thing is understood to be signified, i.e., "*a something*". Under the second reading of *tode ti*, then, our attention is being drawn to a generalized mention of a thing ("*this*") and its kind or genus ("*a something*"). That is, *tode ti* might be taken to mean "something in the class of things which can be pointed out by means of the demonstrative 'this' (see Smith 1921, 19).

The second issue concerns the ambiguity of what the *todi ti* expression is used to indicate. Aristotle commonly uses *tode ti* to indicate substance but he also uses it to indicate non-substances. At *Topics* 116a23, for instance, Aristotle says that

> that [thing] which is essentially so (*to tode ti*) is more desirable than that which does not come within the genus—e.g. justice than a just man; the former falls within the genus, whereas the other does not. (trans. Pickard-Cambridge, modified)

What *tode ti* refers to here is not a substance, but a quality, "justice". So in the case of interpretations (a) and (b), the item in question might be either a substantial or non-substantial entity. The question of which it is, is itself parasitic on the question of the ontological status of relatives: Should we regard relatives as non-instantiated, non-substantial metaphysical entities or as instantiated relational entities? Are relatives metaphysical attributes or concrete items? It is not always clear in *Categories* 7 when Aristotle is discussing metaphysical predicates or properties, for example, as opposed to the concrete individuals that possess those properties. Thus, when Aristotle says that if someone knows of a certain thing (*tis tode ti*) that it is one of the relatives that person also knows that toward which it is holding somehow, the thing being known might be any one of a number of relational entities, e.g., concrete relatives, relational properties, and so forth.

The third area of ambiguity concerns the indefinite pronoun '*tis*'. We must decide whether to make much or little of the *tis*. The use of *tis* often serves to emphasize the particularity of an item. For instance, "*tis bous*" typically would indicate a particular cow, not just the genus cow. By "making much" of *tis* I mean preserving its role as an intensifier of *tode ti*.

Now, how should we translate these two expressions—'*tis*' and '*tode ti*'—that Aristotle places together? Our options are these: We could make much of *tis*, translating *tis tode ti* literally as "a particular this something", "a particular kind of thing" or "a particular certain thing". On the other hand, when we make little of the *tis*, we minimize its particularizing function, allowing *tis* instead to operate as a mere indefinite article. In this case, then, we may translate *tis tode ti* as "a this something" or as I have, "a certain thing."

With the above broad sets of distinctions in hand, let us now see what the different approaches yield for interpreting (4)-(6). If we adopt the most general reading of *tis tode ti* and make the class of relational things equally general, say, non-substantial metaphysical predicates, at (4)-(6) Aristotle makes the following claim:

> (4a) For if someone knows of a certain predicate that it is a relational predicate, and (5a) being for them [metaphysical relational predicates] is the same as holding somehow in relation to a thing, (6a) he also knows that toward which it (the relational predicate) is holding somehow. (*Categories* 8a38-8b1)

If we take the more particularized and intensified rendering of *tis tode ti* and make the class of relational things equally particular by being substantial items, then Aristotle is saying:

> (4b) For if someone knows of a particular concrete relative that it is a relative, and (5b) being for them [concrete relatives] is the same thing as holding somehow in relation to a thing, (6b) he also knows that toward which it (the concrete relative item) is holding somehow. (*Categories* 8a38-8b1)

Whichever is the precise point Aristotle makes at (4)-(6), he follows it by restating the knowing definitely criterion negatively:

> (7) if he does not know at all that towards which it is holding somehow, then (8) neither will he know if it is holding somehow towards something. (*Categories* 8b2-3)

It is not immediately obvious which reading, (4a)-(6a) or (4b)-(6b), is more accurate. The decision here is very much dependent on what one takes Aristotle's project to be in the *Categories*: is Aristotle cataloguing words or attributes or concrete items? Is it some combination of the three? For the time being, I will set these questions aside and return to them in Chapter 4. For now, however, we can turn for immediate help in interpreting (4)-(6) by looking at the next passage.

At (9), Aristotle explicitly turns to address particular cases of relatives.

> (9) And regarding particular cases (*tōn kath' hekasta*) this sort of thing is clear. (10) For example, if a person knows definitely of a thing (*tode ti*) that it is double, (11) he knows definitely at once of what it is double. (12) For if a person by no means knows it to be double of something definite, (13) neither will he know at all whether it is double. And similarly, (14) if he also knows that a thing (*tode ti*) is more beautiful, (15) it is also necessary that he know, because of this, what thing it is more beautiful than. (16) (He will not know in an indefinite way that this thing is more beautiful than an inferior thing). (*Categories* 8b3-13)

Given the analysis of *tode ti* sketched above, the things that pass the epistemic test of the knowing definitely criterion are either the relational predicates, such as <u>double</u> and <u>more beautiful</u>, or concrete relational items, such as the thing that is double and the thing that is more beautiful. Yet even if we understand the *tis tode ti* at (4) to signify metaphysical predicates, the examples at (10)-(15) suggest that Aristotle is turning to specific, concrete cases and that what must be known definitely are concrete relative items. Here is why.

Because no non-substantial entity existentially exists without also existing in its subject, no non-substantial entity can exist without being ontologically dependent on something else. Since relatives are non-substantial entities the same rule applies to them. We know that Aristotle considers relatives "offshoots" of being in that they do not exist in and of themselves, but are posterior to substance (*Nicomachean Ethics* 1096b21–22). They always exist *as* some other item. What is double is always double *of* something, whether it be café espresso or scoops of ice cream. Thus the concrete double item is not *just* double; it is something that exists instantiated in its subject.

The passage from (9) to (16) leaves little doubt, then, that these test cases involve instantiated relational items, not relational metaphysical predicates or mere properties. For regardless of whether we think non-substantial entities are non-recurrent or recurrent individuals, they are always predicated of things other than themselves. If this is correct, then the knowing definitely criterion presents an epistemic challenge the object of which is to confirm that definite knowledge of a relative entails definite knowledge of that relative's *concrete* correlative. Note that if concrete relatives are the knowing definitely criterion's test cases, this does not solve the question of how to interpret (4)-(6). Certainly (4b)-(6b) is consistent with (9)-(16), for the kind of entity involved in Aristotle's epistemic considerations here are concrete items. But the alternative reading of (4a)-(6a) would also be consistent, for Aristotle then would be moving from a general statement about knowing relatives to examination of an actual case of knowing them. If we think relational entities are properties, for example, there would be no great difficulty in moving from a discussion of knowing definitely a property to examining what it means to know definitely that an individual has a relational property.

Aristotle goes on to say why (16) holds. The reason one does "not know in an indefinite way that one thing is more beautiful than another" is that indefinite knowing is "supposition" (*huplēpsis*), not "knowledge" (*ēpistemē*) (*Categories* 8b10). Because such indefinite knowing is supposition and not knowledge, merely supposing that a thing is so offers no guarantee that that thing is in fact so. For instance, I may suppose that leprechauns exist, but supposing that they do is no assurance that they actually do exist. Likewise, it is no good having a vague sense that a rose is more beautiful than some other rose or some other thing without having in mind the thing with which the rose is being compared. If we only suppose that there is something more beautiful, it might turn out, Aristotle says, that "there is nothing inferior to it" (*Categories* 8b12-13).[16]

Aristotle claims that heads and hands are not the kinds of thing that meet the knowing definitely criterion:

> at least for a head or a hand or any such substance, it is possible that someone will know it—the very thing that it is—definitely, without necessarily knowing that toward which it is spoken. For whose head or whose hand this is it is not possible *(ouk estin)* to know definitely *(eidenai hōrismenōs)*. (8b15-19)

Commentators note a problem here with the text (see Ackrill 1963, 23, n. 1; Mignucci 1986, 121, n. 22). Surely it *is* possible to know to whom a hand belongs. The extant manuscripts all have the same text for *Categories* 8b18-19:

For whose head or whose hand this is it is not possible *(ouk estin)* to know definitely.

Ackrill's (1963, 23) emended text reads:

For whose head or whose hand this is it is *not necessary (ouk anagkaion estin)* to know definitely. (Italics mine)

I have followed Ackrill and inserted "necessary" *(anagkaion)* at *Categories* 8b18 as this at least starts us off with a more plausible text to consider.

Presumably what Aristotle has in mind is a situation where one can come upon a human head and know definitely what it is without having to know to whom it belonged. If you are Madame Lafarge, for instance, you *may* recognize whose head it was that dropped into the basket from the guillotine, but you do not *have* to know whose head it was to know that it was a human head. Thus, if we follow the emendation, what Aristotle is saying is that, with heads and hands, it is not necessary to know their rightful owners in order to know what these items are—not that it is not *possible* to know their rightful owners.

Still, there are many other difficulties with M5. I briefly note some of the difficulties here and treat them in greater detail in Chapter 5. First, the knowing definitely criterion appears to be too strong. It seems reasonable to insist that I cannot know that this dove is "more beautiful" without also knowing what it is more beautiful than (e.g., that blue jay). In other cases, though, it seems unreasonable to insist that I cannot know, say, that Rachel is a mother without also knowing definitely that Nathan is her son. Furthermore, I may be as sure of something's being a head as I am of Rachel's being a mother without needing to identify precisely the correlative items involved—either the body to which the head belonged or Rachel's son.

Second, even if the knowing definitely criterion were completely reasonable, it is not clear just how or why this epistemic criterion helps exclude substance from the category of relational being. Why does the criterion provide a good reason for rejecting heads as relatives while accepting double and more beautiful as relatives?

A further difficulty arises. Aristotle seems willing to have a head legitimately be known apart from its body, i.e., apart from its constitutive, organic complement. We might wonder, as Ackrill (1963, 103) does, whether it is out of character for Aristotle to speculate about substance in this manner as Aristotle's view here appears inconsistent with his views elsewhere. According to *Metaphysics* 1035b23–25, a severed finger of a person's hand is a finger in name only. Aristotle is guided at *Metaphysics* 1035b23–25 by two ideas. First, the idea of the whole being necessarily prior to the part and second, by the idea that things are defined by their function and power. At *Politics* 1253a20–25, he remarks that when a person's body is destroyed (i.e., when a person is dead), "there will be no foot or hand except homonymously." So since a remaining part of the body (e.g., a hand) is no longer capable of functioning, it is as much a hand, Aristotle says, as a "stone hand" (*Politics* 1253a20–22). A human finger must be related to (i.e., be part of) the hand of a living human to be "the very thing that it is." The same applies to heads: For a head to exist and be what it is, it must exist as part of a live body.

In addition to the passages from the *Metaphysics* and the *Politics*, Ackrill (1963, 103) cites *De Anima* 412b20–22 and alludes to, but does not cite, *Parts of Animals* 640a35–641a6. These texts and others (e.g., *Generation of Animals* 734b25–27; *Meteorology* 389b30–390a16; *Metaphysics* 1035b23–25) reveal Aristotle's firm stand on the importance of the formal integrity and function of entities, especially human beings. A true (i.e., an actual) human being has an incontrovertible oneness and formal integrity. That is why Aristotle can assert that it is false to say that a dead man is a man (*De Interpretatione* 21a23). Given this stance, it is by no means immediately apparent, then, why Aristotle allows heads and hands to be exempt from the knowing definitely criterion.

2.9 The Sixth Mark of Relatives

Notwithstanding the difficulties just described, on the basis of *E* and the knowing definitely criterion, Aristotle believes he can exclude substance from the category of relation. I will call Aristotle's argument (*Categories* 8a31-8b21) to exclude substance from the category of relation the "substance argument" (SA) and schematize it as follows:

SA1   For something to be a relative, it must be related to something, i.e., it must hold in some way toward something (8a31-33).

SA2   If one knows definitely that a particular thing is a relative, then one also will know definitely that thing to which it is holding somehow (8a37-8b4).

SA3   If one does not know that to which something is related, neither will one know whether it is related to something (8b9).

SA4   One can know definitely that something is a head without having to know that to which it is related (8b15-19).

SA5   Therefore, heads (and other primary substances) are not relatives (8b19-21).

SA6   Since no primary substance is a relative, no secondary substance is a relative either (8a15; see also 2a34–2b5).

SA7   Therefore, no substance is a relative (8b20–21).

We now reach the sixth and last mark of relatives:

M6   No substance is a relative. (8b20)

Aristotle takes the inference from SA1 to SA2 to be valid. The move from SA2 and SA3 is valid as well by *modus tollens*. The inference from SA5 and SA6 to SA7 is valid. SA6 claims that no secondary substance can be a relative if no primary substance is one. This expresses Aristotle's view that it takes the existence of primary substances for the genera of those substances (secondary substances) to exist. But SA2 is problematic for the reasons already discussed, as is SA4. Moreover, before we can accept claims SA3 and SA4 as true, we will have to understand just what it means in this context to know something definitely and why things such as heads and hands do not meet the knowing definitely criterion.

2.10 Summary

As Aristotle's description of relational being and the examples he adduces of it amply illustrate, the view of relation that emerges from *Categories* 7 demonstrates his sense that relation is typically dyadic in nature. His understanding that relatives are dyadically paired items is apparent in three of the six marks of relational being. M3 tells us that every relative is reciprocally related to a correlative (*Categories* 6b28); M4 that most relatives exist simultaneously with their correlatives

(*Categories* 7b15); and M5 that knowing definitely that something is a relative entails knowing definitely that toward which it is "holding somehow" (*Categories* 8a36–37). These marks show that Aristotle thinks of relational being as dyadic being: Relative things are always paired or partnered—conceptually and ontologically—with other things.

Although Aristotle does not state explicitly in *Categories* 7 how items in the category of relation differ ontologically from items in other categories, it is clear that his own paradigmatic meta-ontology is presupposed. He takes the ontological conditions required for monadic subject-predicate and substance-accident relationships and builds on them. His discussion of relatives presumes that relatives and their correlatives have their grounds; it presumes that relatives and correlatives "piggyback", as it were, on primary substance and other predicaments. But this sort of monadic relationship between a relational accident and its subject is not what Aristotle focuses on. What interests Aristotle is not the monadic, but instead the undeniably *dyadic*, character of relational being.

E most reflects Aristotle's treatment of the metaphysical aspects of the category of relation. *E* and its two components reveal Aristotle's understanding of the incompleteness of relations, i.e., that relational being involves one thing's standing somehow in relation to another thing. In Part Two I work out the interpretation of the "holding somehow" component of *E* more fully.

Aristotle clearly understands that what makes both *E*- and *L*-relative entities relational is that they are conceived of with respect to something else and must therefore point to or somehow be related to that other thing. As his examples in *Categories* 8b4–15 show, Aristotle's view is that whenever a particular relational item exists, its correlative must exist also. In short, Aristotle understands that from a pragmatic point of view, to speak of an actual relative is to be speaking of one of at least a dyad of items (i.e., a relative and its reciprocating correlative) that stand in a well-articulated relationship to each other. This view is one reason why Aristotle thinks the knowing definitely criterion follows from *E*. The extent of Aristotle's conception of dyadic relationality, how well he articulates it, and the many epistemological puzzles surrounding it are also addressed in Part Two.

Categories 7 provides a good view of the fundamental elements of Aristotle's relational theory. Aristotle's task of delimiting the category calls on him to do several things at once. He must establish what will constitute the metaphysical parameters of relational being. In addition, he must work out how this conception plays out pragmatically with respect to actual, concrete relational entities. As we will see in Chapter 3, Aristotle's treatment of the category of relation in *Metaphysics* V.15 builds on aspects of his account in the *Categories* but departs from it significantly in tone and emphasis.

Chapter 3

Metaphysics V.15

In this chapter, I present an exegesis of *Metaphysics* V.15. Throughout, I explore the relational theory Aristotle develops and highlight difficulties in the text, returning to them in Part Two. Aristotle uses the same expression he did in the *Categories*—*ta pros ti*—to indicate the subject matter of the text, but there are interesting and significant differences between the two texts. For one thing, the somewhat pedantic tone Aristotle displayed in *Categories* 7 with his treatment of the features of relational being is replaced by a sparse, and in places, more sophisticated approach. This time around he focuses primarily on kinds of relations and much less on the particular and peculiar characteristics of relational being itself. This change in emphasis is noticeable in the way Aristotle groups and re-groups relatives throughout the chapter, each time according to a slightly different classificatory schema.

3. The First Classification Scheme: *Metaphysics* 1020b26–1021a26

Aristotle begins the first classification scheme with a survey, as though exhaustive, of what sorts of things are relative:

Some things are called relative as double is relative to half and triple
relative to a third, and in general multiple to submultiple and that
which exceeds relative to that which is exceeded; others as that which
can heat is relative to the heatable and that which can cut is relative to
the cuttable, and in general that which is able to act to that which is
acted upon; and others as the measurable is relative to the measure, and
the knowable relative to knowledge, and the perceptible relative to
perception. (*Metaphysics* 1020b26–1020b31)

Aristotle initially divides relatives, then, into three classes: (1)
numerical relatives indicative of ratios or proportions, for example, as
double is relative to half, (2) *functional* relatives indicative of active or
passive capabilities or actualizations, for example, as that which can
heat is relative to the heatable; and (3) what I will call *intentional*
relatives, i.e., the relatives as the measurable is to the measure, and so
forth. Aristotle gives a clear indication of what to name the first two
classes of relatives, but he does not do so for the third. Perhaps this is
why the third class assumes different names in the literature. For
instance, Weinberg offers several names for them: "intentional,"
"noetic," or "cognitive" relatives. One reason for calling them
"intentional" relations is that this captures Aristotle's view that the
thinkable, for example, is relative only because something is relative to
it; namely, some act of the mind.[17]

3.1 Numerical Relatives: *Metaphysics* 1020b32–1021a14

At *Metaphysics* 1020b32 Aristotle gives his account of numerical
relatives:

The first sort of relatives are numerically related according to either a
rough or a definite relation, either to them or to 1, e.g., the double bears
a definite numerical relation to 1; that which is many times as great is
related to 1, but not in a definite relation, i.e., not in this or that relation
to 1; 1½ is related to its reciprocal by a definite number relative to a
number; that which is one-and-a-bit is related to its reciprocal by an
indefinite number, just as the multiple is related to 1. The exceeding is
completely numerically indefinite to the exceeded; for number is
commensurate, and number is not said of the incommensurate, but the
exceeding is, relative to the exceeded, so much and something more,
but this "something more" is indefinite; for it can happen to be either
equal or not equal. All these relatives, then, are called numerical
relatives and expressed numerically.... (*Metaphysics* 1020b32–1021a9)

Aristotle describes five kinds of numerical relatives. Below I give an overview of the paradigm Aristotle uses to distinguish the ratio after which I discuss the first four ratios. I follow this with a discussion of the fifth ratio, which is a special case of the fourth type of ratio.

Aristotle chooses two means to note the kinds of relationships numerical relations have: first, the specificity with which the relationship between the terms can be given, and second, the nature of the terms themselves. These form the basis for his paradigm of numerical relations or ratios. First, the numerical ratio may be a numerical designation that is either (a) indefinite or rough or (b) definite or specific. Second, the ratio may involve either (i) numbers other than one or (ii) numbers relative to one (*Metaphysics* 1020b32–33). The ratios, then, are based on the following relationships. I follow Ross's designations for the paradigm (Ross 1924a, 327):

(a, i)   a number's indefinite relation to a number other than one
(a, ii) a number's indefinite relation to one
(b, i)   a number's definite relation to a number other than one
(b, ii) a number's definite relation to one

We notice immediately that Aristotle sanctions indefinite relations. According to *Categories* 7, however, relatives cannot be relative to some unspecified correlative and they cannot be known indefinitely. So what does Aristotle mean here by "indefinite" (*ouk hōrismenon*)?

Ross thinks 'indefinite' pertains to the unspecified terms in a ratio, and 'definite' to its specified terms (Ross 1924a, 328). The distinction Aristotle makes, Ross says, is between ratios expressible by means of a variable, say, *n*, and those expressible with a definite number. Heath agrees, and suggests the indefiniteness refers to the number's being "undetermined" in that it could be any number (Heath 1949, 210).

In this passage Aristotle describes the indefinite portions of the ratios in words that denote the relative's non-specific and indeterminate value. The Greek is crystalline and Aristotle's accompanying examples are clear. By *Categories* 7 standards, though, it hardly seems possible for the terms of numerical ratios to be indefinite (i.e., to be undetermined or unspecified) and still count as relatives. I will take up this problem of reconciling the two accounts later in Part Two.

The First Four Ratios

For now, I move on to the examples Aristotle gives of the ratios. First, there is the relation of the double to its half, i.e., a ratio of 2:1. Since both terms of the ratio are specified numbers, the ratio is a definite numerical relation to one (*Metaphysics* 1020b33). Second, there is the relation of a multiple to its reciprocal. This ratio is an indefinite relation of a number to one, i.e., n:1 (*Metaphysics* 1020b34–1021a1). The ratio is indefinite, Aristotle explains, because it is determined "not by any definite number such as *this* or *this*," but by n, an unspecified number. Third, is the relation of "one-and-a-half to its reciprocal by a definite number relative to a number," i.e., a ratio of 3:2 (*Metaphysics* 1021a1–3). And fourth, there is the ratio of a number and $1/n^{\text{th}}$ of itself (where n is an integer) relative to itself in an indefinite relation. Aristotle describes this ratio as "the one-and-a-bit to one," i.e., $1 + \frac{1}{n} : 1$ or $n + 1 : 1$,

whose reciprocal is or $\dfrac{1}{1 + \frac{1}{n}}$ or $\dfrac{n}{n+1}$ (*Metaphysics* 1021a4).

The following table represents the first four ratios:

Definite and indefinite numerical relations

	Definite	Indefinite
Relative to one	2:1	n:1
Relative to itself	3:2	$n + 1$:n

The Fifth Ratio

Aristotle indicates a fifth, and still more indefinite relationship than the fourth ratio designated by $n + 1$:n. In this ratio "the exceeding is completely numerically indefinite to the exceeded" (*Metaphysics* 1021a5; see also *Physics* 200b28). Aristotle says that one term may exceed the other by "so much and something again," making a relation of "so much and something again:so much" ($n + m : n$). Aristotle uses the notion of incommensurability to explain why the ratio is so indefinite:

> for number is commensurable, and number is not said of the incommensurable; but that which exceeds is, in relation to that which is exceeded, so much and something more; and this something is

indefinite; for it can, indifferently, be either equal or not equal to that which is exceeded. (*Metaphysics* 1021a5–7)

Rational numbers, including integers and fractions, are commensurables; irrational numbers (i.e., numbers that are not the quotients of two integers) are incommensurables.

Aristotle may view the incommensurability as something existing between the terms, e.g., √2:1. Heath gives an example of what this could be. The diagonal of a square exceeds the sides of the square and the excess has to the side a relationship, Heath says, "that cannot be expressed as a ratio between numbers" (Heath 1949, 411).

We would call this ratio an irrational number. However, at *Metaphysics* 1092b19–20 Aristotle says that "a number, whatever it is, is always a number *of* certain things, either of fire or earth or of units." Aristotle's opinion is that incommensurables—which we think of as irrational numbers—are not numbers because they are not numbers *of* anything. We today regard irrationals as numbers, but Aristotle did not. Aristotle does recognize that there are "irrationals"; he just does not think of them as numbers.

Relatives with Respect to "One"

In addition to the above five kinds of numerical relatives, Aristotle places "the equal," "the similar," and "the same" in the class of numerical relatives because they are called what they are with respect to one (*Metaphysics* 1021a8-1021a14). Aristotle makes the same point at *Metaphysics* 1016b17–31 and *Metaphysics* 1052b20–27. In the latter text he says, "That by which each thing is known is called a measure. The measure is one—whether in length, breadth, depth, weight, or speed." Aristotle says that "things are the same whose substance is one, similar whose quality is one, equal whose quantity is one" (*Metaphysics* 1021a10–12). Here are some examples of what Aristotle means.

Take, for example, two books sitting on my desk, both composed of paper, glue, and ink. Even though the books are not one in number, they are the same in substance by virtue of their having one common material composition and one common function. A yellow lemon and a yellow legal pad are similar in that their quality, i.e., their being yellow, is one. And the bag of pistachio nuts in the kitchen cupboard and the box of paper clips in the office are equal in that by one measure their quantity, i.e., their respective weights, is one. In each case the relatives bear a particular relationship to one. Since one is the "measure of number" or principle of measurement (*Metaphysics* 1052b20), Aristotle includes the equal, the similar, and the same under numerical relatives.[18]

We see that the dyadic nature of relatives continues to be central to Aristotle's treatment of the category of relation. This is evident in his view that numerical relatives involve two terms whose relationship typically can be given as a ratio. Aristotle sees that numerical relatives are dyadically related to each other and this informs his treatment of numerical relationships according to the paradigm at *Metaphysics* 1020b32–33. Furthermore, it is clear that by including relations of sameness, equality, and similarity in the class of numerical relatives, Aristotle regards these relatives as pairs or dyads of items since these relations generally involve two or more different terms. I say "generally" because the relation of sameness could involve one term's relationship to itself.

3.2 Functional Relatives: *Metaphysics* 1021a14–25

Aristotle next turns to the second class of relatives, the functional relatives, and continues to treat the relatives as dyadic pairs. He introduces the class by saying that "[t]he active and passive are relative either as potentially active or passive or as actually so" (*Metaphysics* 1021a14). A relative in this class, then, is indicative of the functioning of a thing in two general ways: (1) as an agent and a patient and (2) as a thing having the potential to do something or have something done to it and its actually functioning in this capacity. Aristotle gives some examples.

What is capable of heating is relative to what is capable of being heated because the former *can* heat the latter. Similarly, that which cuts is relative to that which is being cut in that each is actually functioning. Aristotle does not mention here that functional relatives have converses, for example, that the thing which is being cut is relative to that which is cutting it. He does make this point, though, at *Physics* 200b28–32. There he discusses the relationship between agent and patient, and gives examples of the kinds of things that are called relative (e.g., what can cause motion and what can be moved), and their converses (i.e., what can be moved is relative to what can cause movement).

All the functional relatives have an aspect of temporality, i.e., priority and posteriority, about them. What can heat and what can be heated indicate some future functioning; what is cutting now and what is being cut expresses a present functioning; and, as Aristotle states, "that which has produced is relative to what has been produced," marking a past functionality (*Metaphysics* 1021a21–23). The example of the relation of father and son illustrates this:

> For a father is called father of his son in this way; for one of them is a thing that has produced and the other a thing that has been affected. (*Metaphysics* 1021a23–24)

Aristotle ends his discussion of the class by including relatives that indicate the privation of a capacity. "Finally, there are relations according to a privation of a capacity, i.e., the incapable, and those things conceived of in this way, e.g., the invisible" (*Metaphysics* 1021a25–26). Ross suggests that Aristotle is thinking of a relationship between a thing that cannot do something and what it is that it cannot do (Ross 1924a, 330). Aristotle writes, '*to aoraton*', which is translated "the unseen" or "the invisible," suggesting a relation between, e.g., "that which cannot see" and "that which cannot be seen." Aristotle makes a similar point in *Metaphysics* 1019b16–21 where he says that incapacity is the privation of capacity, and that there is a corresponding incapacity to every capacity.

Aristotle counts functional relatives as relatives because they involve causal relationships, but he does not explain in this passage how causal relations work. We can demonstrate how Aristotle's relational and causal theories adjoin, however, by taking his example of that which is heating (*A*) and that which is being heated (*B*), along with other examples.

What happens when *A*, the agent, causes *B*, the patient, to become heated? Once *A* affects *B*, *B* changes from being a "heatable" to a "heated." *B* changes from what only had the *potential* to become heated, to something that *actually* is being heated. Now this change from potentiality to actuality results in an alteration in *B*, the patient. It is an actualization that occurs *in B*.

Here is another example, this time from the *Physics*. Aristotle says that:

> Teaching is the activity of a person who can teach, yet the operation is performed *in* something—it is not cut off from a subject, but is the operation *of* one thing performed *in* another. (*Physics* 202b6–7; see also *Posterior Analytics* 93a1)

Both items are functioning, (teacher and student, the heating and the heated) but for Aristotle, it is in the patient, *B*, that the actual functioning of the agent, *A*, takes place (see also *De Anima* II.2 and *Physics* III.1–3). His view is that although the teacher is teaching and the student is learning, the actual functioning of the teacher—her teaching—takes place *in* the student. The actualization, therefore, occurs in only one item (the student) and is an attribute of that item.

Weinberg states that although Aristotle conceives of causal capacities as relatives or relational entities, Aristotle's theory of causality is proof that his relational theory is not dyadic. Let us pause to examine Weinberg's point.

Weinberg 1965, 70 notes that in the *Physics* and *De Anima*, Aristotle maintains that the realization of the agent is in the patient. What this implies is that causal relations appear to be treated as actualizations of the potency in the patient. Weinberg sees this as allowing the relation to be "absorbed, so to speak, into one of its terms." Thus, Aristotle achieves certain "specious advantage" in Weinberg's estimation by treating the definition of an "attribute so that it contains the nature of the cause of the attribute."

A case in point, Weinberg remarks, is Aristotle's definition of an eclipse of the moon. The eclipse is an accident of the moon and, on Aristotle's view, contains the cause of the deprivation of light the moon suffers.

I agree with Weinberg that Aristotle's causal theory demands that the actualization, i.e., "the acting-and-being-acted-upon" (*De Anima* 426a9), is found in the patient. Nevertheless, Aristotle continually stresses that the actualization requires a fulfillment of two things (agent and patient), both of which must have different definitions. He says:

> Thus there is a single actuality of both agent and patient alike, just as one to two and two to one are the same interval . . . these are one and the same, even though their definitions are not one. (*Physics* 202a18)

It is significant that Aristotle recognizes that agent and patient have two different definitions because this shows that he thinks of agent and patient as two fundamentally different things. So even though Aristotle posits the actuality of one thing within the other, his statements indicate that he does not conflate or confuse agent and patient, or ignore the fact that there is a relation between the two. Aristotle says:

> To generalize, teaching is not the same as learning, or agency as patiency, in the complete sense, even though they belong to the same subject, i.e., the motion; for the actualization of this thing in that and

the actualization of that thing through the action of this differ in definition. (*Physics* 202b19–22)

If Aristotle's causal theory fails adequately to describe causal relations as relations *between* two things, it is not because of a conceptual limitation inherent in his relational theory to consider agent and patient as two distinct entities. Thus far we see Aristotle firmly committed to the view that relation is, at the very least, dyadic in nature. So rather than give Aristotle a "specious advantage," I believe Aristotle's comments on causality reveal how his relational theory may, in a way, outstrip his causal theory by doing a better job of articulating the genuinely dyadic nature of the terms of relations than he does when it comes to explaining his causal theory.

3.3 Intentional Relatives: *Metaphysics* 1021a26–1021b2

Aristotle summarizes the above findings about numerical and functional relatives and moves on to discuss the third class of relatives.

> Numerical and capacity relatives are all relatives because they refer to other things, not because other things refer to them. But the measurable and the knowable and the thinkable are called relative because another thing is relative to it. (*Metaphysics* 1021a26–29)

What Aristotle means when he says that relatives in the former two classes "refer to other things" is that these relatives all relate or refer to their respective correlatives. That is, the relative (i.e., referent) is related to its correlative (i.e., referendum), and the correlative is related to the relative. For example, the double is relative to the half, and the half is relative to the double. Similarly, the scissors doing the cutting are relative to the paper being cut, and the paper being cut is relative to the scissors that are cutting. Both terms of numerical and functional relations are related to each other, and both have their converses.

Relatives in the third, or intentional, class of relatives are different. The perceptible and the thinkable are relative only because something (e.g., sight or thought) refers to it, not because it refers to something else. Aristotle's view here is that as relatives, knowledge, thought, and the others are relative to their respective objects in the way in which numerical or functional relatives are related to their correlatives. Knowledge is relative by its being *of* a particular subject matter just as the double is relative by being double *of* its half.

Because the thinkable and the perceptible are relational in way in which thought and sight are not, they may be said to have an asymmetric character. But with these intentional relations we must be careful not to confuse the asymmetry of the two relatives (e.g., the thinkable and that which is thinking) with a relation itself being asymmetrical.

Most of the relatives Aristotle mentions in the chapter are relatives involved in asymmetrical relations, for example, if *x* is related to *y* by the is cutting relation, *y* has the relation is being cut to *x*, and does not have the is cutting relation to *y*. The only relations that are not asymmetrical that Aristotle mentions, or that are not implied by the relatives he mentions here, are those of sameness, similarity, and equality (*Metaphysics* 1021a9–1021a14). For example, if *z* has a relation of sameness to *y*, then *y* also shares the sameness relation to *z*.

Thought and perception are relations involving a subject and an object: a thing thinking and a thing thought, and so forth. But the object of thought is not a relation. But as Aristotle sets out to explain in this passage, the object of thought—"thinkables"—*are* relatives. The reason that thinking is asymmetrical is that there are instances in which *A* thinks of *B* but *B* does not think of *A*. One way that Aristotle proposes to contrast numerical and functional relatives from intentional ones, then, appears to be based on this asymmetry. This seems to be the kind of asymmetry that emerges in the *Categories* 7 account of some of the same asymmetric relational pairs (e.g., the knowable and knowledge, and the perceptible and perception).

According to *Categories* 6b35–37, knowledge and the knowable are relatives because they meet the criteria of the first account, the *L* formulation of relational being. But the reason why each is a relative is slightly different. Knowledge is a relative because it is *of* something, e.g., American history. The knowable is relative by its being known. That is, something is related to *it*; namely, knowledge. Thus the knowable is a relative in some other way besides being called *of* or *than* something.

Now when Aristotle says (*Metaphysics* 1021a28–29) that "the measurable and the knowable and the thinkable are called relative because another thing is relative to it," he seems poised to make the same point. The knowable is relative by its being known, and now at *Metaphysics* 1021a29, that the thinkable is relative "because another thing"—thought—"is relative to it." But Aristotle continues after *Metaphysics* 1021a29 by stressing another point. Below, with each phrase labeled, is Aristotle's further explanation of what makes intentional relatives relational:

> (a) For 'thinkable' signifies that thought of it is possible, (b) but the thought is not relative to that of which it is a thought (c) (for then we should have said the same thing twice). Similarly, (d) sight is the sight of something, (e) not that of which it is the sight (even though it is true to say that). Rather, (f) sight is relative to color or to another thing such as this. (g) But the other way of speaking would be to say the same thing twice: (h) 'sight is of that of which sight is'. (*Metaphysics* 1021a31–1021b3)

Let me quickly sketch out what Aristotle is doing here, before moving on to examine the passage more closely. *Metaphysics* 1021a31–1021b3 purports to be an explanation of what accounts for the asymmetrical character of the thinkable in relation to thought, and the perceptible in relation to sight. Aristotle gives two examples of how to define each member of the pairs. He clearly thinks that there is a right way and a wrong to define both thought and sight; the wrong way is to give a definition that amounts to "saying the same thing twice." As we shall see, the argument Aristotle presents is fraught with ambiguity. Before proceeding with the analysis of the argument, we need to be aware of what these ambiguities are.

The Two Ambiguities

There are two areas of ambiguity that make interpreting the passage difficult. The first is the ambiguity of the passage's verbal adjectives. This is the same problem we encountered in *Categories* 6b35 ff. Verbal adjectives can have the force in the Greek of a perfect passive participle as in "the loved" or they may carry the force of possibility as in "the lovable." The passage at *Metaphysics* 1021a29–30 has three verbal adjectives: '*to metrēton*', '*to epistēton*', and '*to dianoēton*', which I have translated with the sense of possibility, i.e., as "the measurable," "the knowable," and "the thinkable," respectively. The first two of these adjectives also appear at the beginning of the chapter (*Metaphysics* 1020b31–32) in Aristotle's initial three examples of intentional relatives: '*to metrēton*', '(*to*) *epistēton*', and '(*to*) *aisthēton*'. I have translated these "the measurable," "the knowable," and "the perceptible." However, the ambiguity of the adjectives leads us to wonder whether Aristotle may instead have in mind, e.g., "the measured" or "the known," in the sense that these are things that have been measured or known. How this further affects our interpretation of the passage I will note in a moment.

In addition to the ambiguity of the verbal adjectives, the verb "to be" at *Metaphysics* 1021a31, conjugated and accented as '*estin*' (ἔστιν) invites and encourages ambiguity. The verb has the meaning of the "is" of existence, as in "to exist," but the verb also carries the sense of possibility as in "it is possible." Smyth 1983, 43, 187.b notes that as accented here *esti(n)* may express existence or possibility. So we must surmount a double hurdle: Do the verbal adjectives carry the force of the perfect past participle or of possibility, and what sense of "is" is at play?

How we resolve these ambiguities affects our interpretation of Aristotle's argument at *Metaphysics* 1021a30–1021b3. Let us briefly examine just the initial two phrases of this passage, the ones I have labeled (a) and (b), so we may better see the stakes before us. Four interpretive options available to us. Below, I state each of them in a way that explicitly emphasizes the different options.

(A)   If X is a thinkable this signifies that there exists thought of X.

(A*)   If X is a thinkable this signifies that thought of X is possible.

(B)   If X is a thought thing this signifies that there exists thought of X.

(B*)   If X is a thought thing this signifies that thought of X is possible.

I start by examining the ambiguity of the verb "to be." Options (A*) and (B*) reflect the "is" of possibility. (A*) says that if a thing is thinkable, then thought of it is possible, too. (B*) says that if X has been thought of, the thought of it is possible. In (A) and (B), we have the existential sense of "is." (A) and (B) suggest that the thinkable or the thought thing are relative because the thinkable and thought of it exist simultaneously. In the case of (A), this means that without being thought of, X cannot be a thinkable. Similarly, with (B), X cannot be a thought thing without there simultaneously being thought of X. In other words, with options (A) and (B), there must be concurrent, simultaneous thought of X for it to be a thinkable.

One thing that this ambiguity reveals is that Aristotle may want to explain the asymmetric character of intentional relatives by appealing to the lack of simultaneity these relatives and correlatives have. This again is reminiscent of another approach he used to explain the asymmetry of these relatives. At *Categories* 7b15 ff., after explaining that most relatives are simultaneous by nature, Aristotle accounts for the asymmetrical character of knowledge and the knowable by describing the lack of simultaneity between them. He says (*Categories* 7b25–26) that "the knowable would seem to be prior to knowledge" because it is of "already existing things that we acquire knowledge." This means that the knowable is not existentially dependent on my having knowledge of it. Aristotle can account for the asymmetric character of the relatives by the temporal priority of the knowable and by an accompanying lack of simultaneity between knowledge and the knowable. He may intend to do the same thing here in *Metaphysics* V.15 and say that the thinkable is existentially prior to, and not dependent upon, my thought of it.

Kirwan complains, though, that Aristotle's comments at *Metaphysics* 1021a32 mar the point concerning the lack of simultaneity these relatives have (Kirwan 1971, 166). Kirwan translates "*to te gar dianoēton sēmainei hoti estin autou dianoia*" (*Metaphysics* 1021a31) as "[f]or 'thinkable' signifies that there *exists* thought of it."[19] Based on Kirwan's translation, Aristotle's point here would be that there is an existential simultaneity between the referent and the referendum. Such a view, of course, would be completely opposed to the position Aristotle takes at *Categories* 7b15–8a12, and Kirwan chides Aristotle for spoiling that text's application here: Clearly a thing *can* be a thinkable without there being thought of it. It is Kirwan's strong existential rendering of '*estin*' that makes the error apparent. However, given the grammatical context of *Metaphysics* 1021a32, we can translate *estin* in the weaker sense of possibility as I have done: [f]or 'thinkable' signifies that thought of it is possible." My translation addresses the verbal ambiguity in one way; Kirwan's seizes upon another way. My translation leaves open the possibility that Aristotle means to adopt the view of the asymmetry he described at *Categories* 7b15 ff. Which view is Aristotle asserting?

Kirwan cites *De Anima* III.2 as evidence of a potential source of confusion about Aristotle's position on the existential simultaneity of these relatives. At *De Anima* 425b26–426a26, Aristotle considers the simultaneity of the perceptible with respect to perception. He distinguishes between an actual sound (or an object that is capable of sounding), on the one hand, and actual hearing on the other. Aristotle's example is of someone who has hearing but is not hearing at the present time. However, when both things are actualized (i.e., when a bell actually is ringing and a person actually is hearing the bell), both things occur simultaneously (*De Anima* 425b30–426a1). That is, both are "simultaneously destroyed and simultaneously preserved" (*De Anima* 426a15–19). In the strict sense, then, the actual object of perception exists simultaneously with the act of perception, such that if there is no perception, there is no perceptible. The passage supports Kirwan's translation: the perceptible signifies that there *actually is* perception of it.

I agree that Aristotle makes this point in *De Anima* III.2, but it is not his sole point. Aristotle says that the perceptible and perception are spoken of in two ways: In terms of the potentiality and actuality of perception, and in terms of the potentiality and actuality of the perceptible. According to *De Anima* 426a15–25, the potentially perceptible object exists prior to perception. "The earlier students of nature were mistaken in their view," Aristotle says, "that without sight there was no white or black, without taste no savour" (*De Anima* 426a20, trans. Smith). The red apple on the table exists as a potential object of perception. As an actual perceptible, however, the apple exists as an actual object of perception when perception and the perceptible exist simultaneously. A detailed examination of Aristotle's various accounts of perception is beyond the scope of our concerns here, but what the above passages reveal is that Aristotle does qualify his view that perceptibles exist simultaneously. This means we can put the ambiguity of the Greek and the alternative views available to us to our advantage and translate this section of *Metaphysics* V.15 in a way that makes it more compatible with *Categories* 7 and *De Anima* III.2 accounts of perception.[20] Now that we have a grasp of the ambiguities of the passage, we will have a better start evaluating Aristotle's explanation of the asymmetrical character of intentional relatives.

The Examples of Thought and Sight: Metaphysics 1021a31–1021b3

I repeat below the reasoning Aristotle offers to explain the asymmetrical nature of intentional relatives:

(a) For 'thinkable' signifies that thought of it is possible, (b) but the thought is not relative to that of which it is a thought (c) (for then we should have said the same thing twice). Similarly, (d) sight is the sight of something, (e) not that of which it is the sight (even though it is true to say that). Rather, (f) sight is relative to color or to another thing such as this. (g) But the other way of speaking would be to say the same thing twice: (h) 'sight is of that of which sight is'. (*Metaphysics* 1021a31–1021b3)

Let us begin by examining the first example, that of the thinkable and thought. Aristotle contends that the thinkable is a relative because something is relative to it, not because the thinkable is related to something (*Metaphysics* 1021a29–30). And so he says that:

(1)   'Thinkable' signifies that thought of it is possible. [from (a)]

Now whether the thinkable is something actually thought of, or potentially thought of, something is thinkable because it is able to be thought of. Take a circle. A circle is a thinkable because it is able to be thought of, and because of this, we can say that a circle is a thinkable in relation to thought. So from (1) we can infer (2):

(2)   The thinkable is somehow in relation to thought.

Since thought is *of* something, and since the thinkable is a relative because thought is able to be *of* it, one might understandably suppose that:

(3)   Thought is relative to the thinkable.

Someone attempting to spell (3) out further, might even venture to put it this way as I have in (4):

(4)   Thought is relative to that of which it is a thought. [from negation of (b)]

It is easy to see, then, how one could arrive from (1) to (4). But while Aristotle affirms (1), he rejects (4), saying that

(5)   Thought is not relative to that of which it is a thought. [from (b)]

But why does Aristotle reject (4)? Not because (4) is false, as Aristotle himself remarks a bit later (*Metaphysics* 1021b1). Rather, he thinks that:

(6)   (4) amounts to saying the same thing twice. [from (c)]

It is hard to tell from Aristotle's somewhat cryptic comments here why he thinks the practice of "saying the same things twice" should be avoided. In *Sophistical Refutations* 173b10–11, however, Aristotle discusses what it means to "say the same thing twice" and uses the expression "snub nose" to explain the prohibition against uttering a redundancy. "Snubness" is concavity of the nose. Note that the word 'nose' already included in the definition of snubness. So when we say "snub nose," we repeat ourselves by saying, in effect, "snub nose nose." The prohibition's application here, with respect to thought, is that one component of the definition is repeated such that the content or object of thought is not indicated. Simply saying that a thought is "that of which it is a thought" does nothing to identify what is the content of the thought. One might as well define thought by saying: "thought is thought of a thought." Or to put it more crudely: "thought is thought thought." So in terms of identifying what thought is, (4) is as redundant as saying "nose nose." That is why in saying something twice (e.g., "thought thought," "sight sight") we fail to define or identify that item properly. As Kirwan remarks (1971, 166), from Aristotle's perspective (4) is an "unhelpful" thing to say because (4) cannot serve to identify anything as a thought. Indeed, it serves to lull us into uttering a tautology. In order to identify a thought properly, one must give the subject matter or content of the thought. For example, we should identify a thought as the thought that Los Angeles is east of Reno, or the thought that the key of C-sharp minor has only four sharps.

In the example of sight (*Metaphysics* 1021a33–1021b3), Aristotle continues along the same lines as above. He says that:

(7)   Sight is sight of something. [from (d)]

For example, sight must be of color or some other such thing. Continuing on, Aristotle says that:

(8)   Sight is not that of which it is the sight. [from (e)]

What Aristotle denies here is that:

(9)   Sight is that of which it is the sight. [from negation of (e)]

Even though (9) is true (*Metaphysics* 1021b1), it is a tautology. For Aristotle, it is better to say that:

(10) Sight is relative to color (and other things such as color).
      [from (f)]

Aristotle rejects (9) because it does an inadequate job of saying what sight is, just as (4) does a poor job articulating what thought is. The reason he gives, as before, is that:

(11) (9) amounts to saying the same thing twice. [from (g)]

That is, (9) is the same as trying to define sight by saying that:

(12) Sight is the sight of that which is the object of sight.
      [from (h)]

When we define sight or thought in the ways Aristotle rejects, we hopelessly spin our wheels, never getting to the task of defining or identifying the item. Instead, when we identify the objects of sight, thought, and so forth, these must be stated so that when we say what a thought is, for instance, we give what is the content of that thought.

Has Aristotle distinguished intentional relatives from other relatives? Does Aristotle's explanation give a satisfactory account of the asymmetric character of relatives in the third class? For Morales, the asymmetrical character of relatives is evident in light of the existential autonomy and the definitional or logical priority of relatives in this class (Morales 1994, 268–70). Morales's view is that Aristotle accepts the *Categories* 7 position that knowables exist prior to, and have existential autonomy from, knowledge of whatever is knowable. On this account, the knowable can exist without being related in any way to knowledge, whereas relatives in the other two classes are existentially dependent on each other.

The asymmetric character is further apparent in the logical priority of the knowable over knowledge. This priority occurs, Morales says, because knowledge is determined by what is knowable (Morales 1994, 265). That is, the knowable gives knowledge its specific content.

For example, the knowable (i.e. the object of knowledge), being prior to knowledge, gives knowledge its specific content and may be used to define it: grammar may be defined as (a kind of) "knowledge of letters"; or music as (a kind of) "knowledge of sounds". (Morales 1994, 269)

On Morales's view, then, grammar is a kind of knowledge, a "knowledge of letters." The knowledge of letters is the knowable here, and it is this, the knowledge of letters, that determines the scope of, or defines, what grammar is. Grammar does not determine what knowledge of letters is. And so knowledge, in this case, grammar, is determined by its content or subject matter.

This is the same observation Aristotle makes later at *Metaphysics* 1053a31-33. There he explains that while we may think knowledge and perception are the measure of our knowing things, actually they are the things measured by other things (i.e., knowables and perceptibles). In other words, our knowledge is determined by what is knowable; the knowable is not determined by our knowledge.

While Morales's remarks indicate how Aristotle views the asymmetric character of this class of relatives, I do not believe that Aristotle does such a good job of distinguishing intentional relatives from numerical and functional ones. In the first place, Aristotle's comments at *Metaphysics* 1021a31 ff. do not so much explain what makes the thinkable, for example, an exception to the normative way in which things are relative, as show what is exceptional about thought. The third class supposedly is marked by the non-reciprocity of only one member (i.e., the thinkable) of the relational pair as opposed to the reciprocity of both members the relational pairs in the other classes (e.g., the reciprocity of the double and the half). Yet the third class actually is marked by neither member of the relational pair of intentional relatives being reciprocal.

Ross suggests another way Aristotle fails to distinguish carefully between the three classes. What is supposed to set these relatives apart is the asymmetrical relationship that exists between relatives of the third class, for example, thought and the thinkable. Unlike the relative-correlative pairs double and half, or the thing which cuts and the thing which is being cut, the primary being of the thinkable is not its standing in relationship *to* some other thing. That which is thinkable has "a nature of its own," Ross says, besides being the object of thought (Ross 1924a, 330). But as Ross correctly observes, relatives in the other classes also have this characteristic. According to *Metaphysics* 1088a24 concrete relatives have some primary being or "nature" (to use Ross's terminology) other than their being a relative. As Ross remarks, a relative has "a nature of its own besides being double or half, just as that which is known must have a nature of its own besides being known" (Ross 1924a, 331).

Kirwan also notes that Aristotle does not clearly distinguish the three classes of relatives. For instance, Aristotle's comment about saying the same thing twice applies equally to double or slave as it does to thought (Kirwan 1971, 166). It is just as unhelpful to say that "a slave is a slave of that of which he is a slave," as it is to say that "a thought is relative to that of which it is a thought."

But Kirwan does observe that perhaps the third class of relatives could be distinguished by what appears to be a stronger and weaker sense of being relational. The relatives master and slave, for instance, are identified by reference to the each other. A slave is a slave of a master, and a master is a master of a slave. In contrast, a thought has to be identified by its subject matter, e.g., Greek grammar. But if we identify Greek grammar (i.e., 'the subject matter of a thought') in terms of its being a thought, we wind up with identifying it as "'the subject matter of a thought' of a thought" (Kirwan 1971, 166).

That identifying the relatives results in this difference may represent a weak and a strong sense of what it means to be relational. Kirwan does not flesh out this distinction fully, but I believe what he means is this. Master and slave are weakly relative because they are identifiable as being "of something." Here, as we found with the *L* formulation of relational being in *Categories* 7, being "of something" is enough to qualify a thing as a relative. Thought, however, is relative in the strong sense in that "any description of a thought identifies it only by reference to a different entity, its subject-matter" (Kirwan 1971, 166).

Kirwan mainly is on the right track here, but I do not see that master and slave fit what I think he considers things that are weakly relative. Master and slave are *L*-relative, but they also meet the criteria for being *E*-relative. Second, while a thought does have to be identified as having some subject matter, that subject matter is no less a "different entity," as Kirwan calls it, as is the correlative of a slave or a master.

3.4 The Second Classification Scheme: *Metaphysics* 1021b3–11

Aristotle opens the last portion of the chapter by introducing yet another classificatory schema for relatives.

> Things that are by their own nature called relative are called so sometimes in the above sense, sometimes because the classes that

include them are of this sort, e.g., medicine is thought to be relative because its genus, knowledge, is thought to be relative. Further, there are those things in virtue of which the things that have them are called relative, e.g., equality is relative because the equal is, and likeness because the like is. Other things are relative by accident, e.g., a man is relative because he happens to be double of something and double is a relative term; or the white is relative, if the same thing happens to be double and white. (*Metaphysics* 1021b3–11)

The new scheme makes a broad, twofold division of relatives: (1) some relatives are relative by their nature, i.e., the relatives called relatives "in their own right" (*kath' heauta*) (*Metaphysics* 1021b4); and (2) others are relative only accidentally (*kata sumbebēkos*) (*Metaphysics* 1021b8). Aristotle lists (*Metaphysics* 1021b3–10) three ways relatives are included in the class of relatives that are relative by their nature: (a) "in the above sense," i.e., according to the classificatory schema just presented from *Metaphysics* 1020b26-1021b2 and thus would include numerical, functional, and intentional relatives, (b) when their genera are of those kinds and (c) when their possessors are relative. Those not relative by their own nature are in the second class, those that are accidentally, or coincidentally, relative (*Metaphysics* 1021b11).

3.5 Things Relative by Their Nature: *Metaphysics* 1021b3-8

What are we to make of Aristotle's saying that relatives may be classified as being relatives by their own nature or in their own right? How we should interpret the notion of things being relative "by virtue of themselves" or "in themselves"?
Various texts in which Aristotle addresses either relatives specifically or discusses other predicaments that in some way share features of relatives offer some illumination. In the end, however, these texts, along with the passage here, present a less than clear picture of what constitutes a thing being relational by its nature.

Let us begin with two possible interpretations and examine the textual evidence in support or in opposition to them. One possible interpretation is that a relative in this group is relative in some absolute sense such that it is relative by virtue of itself (*kath' hauto*), i.e., without having to be related to something. Another possibility is that Aristotle wants to say that some things are relatives simply by being the kinds of things that are relational. That is, regardless of the particular ways in which numerical, functional, and intentional relatives exhibit their relationality, they all are by nature relational.

At first glance the former interpretation seems unlikely, especially given Aristotle's emphasis on the necessary correlativity of all relatives. Both the *Categories* 7 and *Metaphysics* V.15 accounts of relational being show that relatives are always conceived of with respect to something. However this first interpretation might be thought to derive some support from the *Metaphysics* account of quantity (*Metaphysics* V.13), where Aristotle contradicts these accounts. He defines quantity as being "that which is divisible into two or more constituent parts of which each is a one and a 'this'" (*Metaphysics* 1020a7-8, trans. Ross). He then distinguishes broadly between things that are quantities in virtue of their own nature (*kath' hauta*) and accidentally (*kata sumbebēkos*) (*Metaphysics* 1020a14–32).

> Again, some things are called quantities in virtue of their own nature, others accidentally, e.g. the line is a quantity (for a certain kind of quantity is present in the formula which states what it is), and others are modifications and states of this kind of being, e.g. much and little, long and short, broad and narrow, deep and shallow, heavy and light, and the other terms of this sort. (*Metaphysics* 1020a14-22, trans. Ross)

He continues:

> And also large and small, and larger and smaller, both in themselves and when taken relatively to each other, are by their own nature attributes of quantity; but these names are transferred to other things also. (*Metaphysics* 1020a23-36)

One surface is larger than some other surface, for example, or one surface is said to be small relative to another surface. Thus those in the former group, i.e., those modifications of substance which in virtue of their own nature are quantities, are understood as being quantities in virtue of their own nature both "in themselves (*kath' hauta*) and when taken relatively to each other (*pros allēla*)" (*Metaphysics* 1020a24, trans. Ross).

Aristotle does not explain what he means by saying that attributes of quantity can be understood in themselves (*kath' hauta*) to be quantities in virtue of their own nature. However, he does explain what he means for a thing to be a quantity "accidentally". Things that belong accidentally in the category of quantity belong because, e.g., the things they are the properties of themselves belong to that category

(*Metaphysics* 1020a26-28). This is why white, for instance, can be called a quantity because the surface it belongs to is a quantity. Aristotle's explanation here mirrors the one he gives at *Metaphysics* V.15 of relatives that are relative by accident. A man is accidentally relative because a property he has, being double, is a relative (*Metaphysics* 1021b8-11).

But what of Aristotle's contention (1020a23) that large and small, and larger and smaller are said to be by their own nature (*kath' hauta*) attributes of quantity both in themselves (*kath' hauta*) and relative to each other (*pros allēla*)? First, we note that in the *Metaphysics* account of quantity Aristotle calls large and small quantities (*Metaphysics* 1020a23), but in the *Categories* account of quantity he calls them relatives (see *Categories* 5b11–29). His rationale for calling them relatives is that they must be taken in reference to something besides themselves in order to be what they are. "For nothing is called large or small just in itself, but by reference to something else" (*Categories* 5b16, trans. Ackrill; see also *Categories* 6a36–37).

The trickier matter rests with what Aristotle means by saying that small or larger are attributes of quantity "in themselves" (*kath' hauto*). Aristotle seems poised to make a distinction between things taken relatively to each other and, in at least some sense, those things considered on their own or absolutely. Since Aristotle offers no explanation here at *Metaphysics* 1020a23 we must look elsewhere for interpretive clues.

Categories 5b11-22 again offers some insight. There Aristotle says that nothing is called large or small just by itself. Thus when a mountain is called small yet a grain of millet large, each is thought to be small or large with respect to other items in its class. Kirwan remarks that Aristotle is distinguishing at *Categories* 5b11 ff. between certain cases in which a statement remains intelligible without having an explicit specification of a correlative context for a relational term (Kirwan 1971, 161-162. See also Bogen 1992, 18). What Kirwan means is that the statement, e.g., "Mt. Hood is small", is intelligible without having to say in what respect Mt. Hood is small, although this information can be specified. The statement "Mt. Hood is smaller" is different. Here 'smaller' has to be taken relatively to something else.

Aristotle makes it clear, though, that if one were to say that a thing could be small in and of itself (*kath' hauto*), a mountain would not be called small absolutely (*Categories* 5b20-22). In other words, in calling the mountain small, one still has to have in mind something in regards to which the mountain can be called small. For example, one might have Mt. Everest in mind when saying that Mt. Hood is small for it is small, compared to Mt. Everest. Hence, on the *Categories* 5 account at least, the lack of a stated correlative does not mean that that which is small is small *absolutely*, i.e., in the strict sense of not needing to be conceived of with respect to some other thing.

It does not seem plausible, then, that with "by their own nature" Aristotle means to say that numerical, functional, and intentional relatives are relatives without regard to any other item or some other thing.

Numerical, Functional, and Intentional Relatives by Their Own Nature

Aristotle may want to call numerical, functional, and intentional relatives relative by their own nature because it is the essence of such things to be relative. When Aristotle speaks of the "essence" of a thing he primarily is interested in substance and examining a 'this'. But he also says that we can ask what is the essence of any of the predicaments.

> '[W]hat a thing is' in one sense means substance and a 'this', in another one or other of the predicates, quantity, quality, and the like. For as 'is' is predicable of all things, not however in the same sense, but of one sort of thing primarily and of others in a secondary way, so too the 'what' belongs simply to substance, but in a limited sense to the other categories. For even of a quality we might ask what it is, so that a quality also is a 'what',—not simply, however, but just as, in the case of that which is not, some say, in the abstract, that that which is not *is*—not *is* simply, but *is* non-existent. So too with quality. (*Metaphysics* 1030a17-27, trans. Ross)

Where does this leave us with regard to this first subclass of things relative by their own nature in *Metaphysics* V.15? What is the "essence" of being relative? We can come to some understanding by looking back to what Aristotle says about *E* relatives in *Categories* 7. There he says that being relative is the same as holding in some way towards something (*Categories* 8a31 ff.). In the *Categories* Aristotle insists that relatives be reciprocally related to their correlatives so that, e.g., what it means to be double is to be twice of the half, and vice versa. But since the criterion of reciprocity is dropped in the *Metaphysics* account of relational being, what remains constant in both accounts is the correlativity of the relatives and the holding somehow toward something. The essential character of relatives, then, would be the same that held in the *Categories* 7 account. If we apply this same interpretation to the *Metaphysics* V.15 account, then numerical relatives such as double or functional relatives such as that which heats are relatives simply by being the kinds of things they are, i.e., by being essentially correlative.

Does this analysis hold true of intentional relatives? One could say that the intentional relatives the thinkable and perceptible are relatives in their own right because they still exhibit correlativity even though they are the very things they are by virtue of having something else be relative to them (*Metaphysics* 1021a29).

Elsewhere, however, Aristotle indicates that intentional relatives are not a part of the class of relatives that are relative by their own nature. At *Metaphysics* X.6 Aristotle distinguishes between the way in which one and number are opposed, not as contraries, but nevertheless as opposed in the way in which intentional relatives are (e.g., the measure and the measurable) (*Metaphysics* 1057a3-5).

> The one is opposed then to the many in numbers as measure to thing measurable; and these are opposed as relatives which are not from their very nature relative. We have distinguished elsewhere the two senses in which relatives are so called—some as contraries, others as knowledge to thing known, a term being called relative because another is relative to it (*Metaphysics* 1056b34-1057a1, trans. Ross.)

Aristotle marks "two senses in which relatives are so called": those that are opposed as contraries and those which are opposed as knowledge is opposed to the thing known. Once again, the distinction is between things that are relative by their own nature and those are not. This time we have this resulting correspondence: Those relatives that are opposed as contraries correspond to things relative by their own nature, and the intentional relatives correspond, as Aristotle has just said, to those relative that are not from their very nature relative.

Aristotle's comment that he has distinguished elsewhere the two senses in which relatives are called relative refers more closely to his discussion of relatives at *Metaphysics* V.15 than to the account at *Categories* 7. This is suggested by the explicit classification at *Metaphysics* V.15 of relatives that are so by virtue of their own nature (*Metaphysics* 1021b3-4), and further by the distinction Aristotle draws at *Metaphysics* V.15 between intentional and non-intentional relatives. Although Aristotle does treat intentional relatives, for example, the knowable and perceptible, in *Categories* 7 (6b33–36, 7b24-27), he plainly states in *Categories* 7 that not all relatives have contraries and lists this fact as the first of six marks of relational being (6b15; see also *Categories* 11b33–36). It seems clear, then, that this particular classification of two senses in which relatives are called relatives—by being contraries and by behaving in the peculiar manner that intentional relatives do—is not modeled after the *Categories* 7 account of relation. Yet even with the close affinity between *Metaphysics* X.6 and *Metaphysics* V.15, there are obvious differences between the texts which impact our analysis of what Aristotle means by calling some things relative "by their own nature."

Aristotle correctly states that there is the sense in which things are relative in the way the knowable and knowledge are related. According to *Metaphysics* 1021a36–b3, the measurable, the knowable, and the thinkable are said to be relative because something is relative to them. But we notice a slight difference between how the idea is presented at *Metaphysics* X.6 and *Metaphysics* V.15. *Metaphysics* X.6 has it that knowledge is a relative because something is relative to *it* (*Metaphysics* 1056b36 and 1057a7–8), instead of what Aristotle has at *Metaphysics* 1021a31, that the knowable is relative because knowledge is related to it. I agree with Ross (1924b, 297) that the disparity can be accounted for by realizing that both knowledge and the knowable can be understood as being prior to the other. Knowledge, in one sense, is prior to the knowable, Ross says, in that the knowable is a potential or possible object of knowledge. In terms of existential priority, though, the knowable exists before knowledge. Whichever is not deemed prior, then, is held to be only incidentally relative, i.e., relative by virtue of something being relative to it.

But Aristotle clearly is wrong and misstates his own view if he means to say that relatives are exclusively opposed to each other as contraries and that this feature exemplifies what it means for a relative to be a relative in virtue of its own nature. Recall that at *Categories* 6b15 Aristotle denies that all relatives have contraries. For example, double is a relative but it has no contrary. Good and bad are contraries of each other but this does not make them relatives. As Aristotle himself notes at *Categories* 11b34-36, "good" is not just what it is *of* its opposite: Good is not called *good* of the bad (*Categories* 11b35) but the contrary of the bad (*Categories* 11b34–36). Thus, as Ross notes, Aristotle imprecisely calls things normative relatives, i.e., things relative by their own nature, when they are opposed as contraries (Ross 1924b, 297).

Given the disparate ways Aristotle categorizes relatives under the classification relatives "by their own nature" and his failure to specify precisely what he means by the notion as it applies to relational being, it is quite difficult to say conclusively why Aristotle places the numerical, functional, and intentional relatives under this classification, or the other subgroups of relatives under this classification. I think the most reasonable analysis, though unavoidably vague, is that each of these relatives, by being what each one is, reflects what it means to be relational. I will apply this interpretation to the remaining members of this class of things relative by their own nature.

Relatives by Nature Because the Genus is Relative

The second subgroup consists of those considered relative by nature because their genus is relative.

> Things that are by their own nature called relative are called so . . . sometimes because the classes that include them are of this sort, e.g. medicine is thought to be relative because its genus, knowledge, is thought to be relative. (*Metaphysics* 1021b3-6, trans. Ross)

Aristotle says that a thing is relative when its genus is included among the relatives. For instance, medicine is a relative because its genus, knowledge, is a relative. His reasoning is that if the genus of a particular species is relative, then every species under that genus is relative, too. Note that this differs in some respects from his comments elsewhere. For instance at *Categories* 8, Aristotle makes it clear that even though the species counts as a relative through the auspices, as it were, of the genus, the species is not actually a relative.

> For knowledge, a genus, is called just what it is, of something else (it is called knowledge of something); but none of the particular cases is called just what it is, of something else. For example, grammar is not called grammar of something nor music music of something. If at all it is in virtue of the genus that these too are spoken of in relation to something: grammar is called knowledge of something (not grammar of something) and music knowledge of something (not music of something). Thus the particular cases are not relatives. (*Categories* 11a24-32, trans. Ackrill)

So while knowledge is a relative, one of its species, grammatical knowledge, is not relative. *Topics* 124b15–22 again emphasizes that by no means is it necessary for a species to be considered relative simply because its genus is.

> If the species is a relative, look to see whether the genus is a relative as well; if the species is a relative, then so too is the genus, e.g., as in the case with <u>double</u> and <u>multiple</u>; for each is a relative. On the other hand, if the genus is a relative, it is not necessary that the species should be so as well; for knowledge is a relative, but grammar is not. (Or possibly not even the first statement would seem to be true; for virtue is essentially noble and essentially good, and yet, while virtue is a relative, good and noble are not relatives but qualities.) (*Topics* 124b15-22)

Relatives by Nature Due to Possession

The last subgroup in the class consists of things, what we call relations, which are relative by nature because the things that possess them and are paronymously named after them are relatives. For example, equality is a *pros ti*, i.e., in this case a relation, because each member of a pair of equals is a relative with respect to the other.

> Furthermore, there are those things in virtue of which the things that have them are called relative, for example, equality is relative because the equal is, and likeness because the like is. (*Metaphysics* 1021b6–8)

Aristotle is not saying that equality possesses equals. Rather, each member of a pair of equals possesses equality with respect to the other. Likewise for paronymy. At *Categories* 1a12-15 it is the concrete γραμματικός who gets his name from the abstract feminie of γραμματική.

3.6 Accidental Relatives: *Metaphysics* 1021b8–11

Aristotle ends the chapter by noting the last classification, things that are relative by accident.

> Some things are relative accidentally, e.g., a man is relative because he happens to be double of something and double is a relative; or the white is relative, if the same thing happens to be double and white. (Metaphysics 1021b8-11)

According to 1021b8–9, we may consider a man to be relative "because he happens to be double of something" (see also Physics 224a19–23). Thus if Nathan is double the size of Ashton, we may say that Nathan is relative. He is relative, not because he is a man, but because he is double the size of Ashton. The relatives in this group encompass relatives Aristotle discusses in his Categories 7 account. For example, it is not by being a biped, or capable of knowledge or even by being man that an individual is a master. A master is a master only if he has a slave (See Categories 7a28-7b1). This last classification of relatives at Metaphysics 1021b8 ff. makes explicit the point that substances which are called relative, are, in fact, only accidentally relative. A slave is every bit as concrete as a man, it is just that Callias is essentially a man but only accidentally a slave.

3.7 Summary

The *Metaphysics* V.15 account of relatives departs significantly from the *Categories* 7 account in structure and focus. The slow, methodical inspection of relational being in *Categories* 7 is gone; in its place is a brisk survey of classes of relational entities. For the most part Aristotle abandons his linguistic approach to characterizing relatives and relational words. The exceptions are three. First, Aristotle does call attention to relations after which relatives are paronymously named (*Metaphysics* 1021b7–8). Second, although he does not explicitly mention it, functioning and the intentional relatives have a difference in verbal ending, a feature that can be a linguistic indicator of relatives (e.g., what is capable of heat-*ing* is relative to what is capable of being heat-*ed*). And third, Aristotle enlists the prohibition against saying the same thing twice in his account of intentional relatives.

The focus shifts, too, from the task of determining the primary formula for relational being to the task of exploring more non-rudimentary properties or features of relatives. In some cases, this involves tacitly building on the findings of *Categories* 7; in other cases, Aristotle abandons some of those same findings. For instance, the reciprocal nature of relational correlatives is one of the key marks of relational being in *Categories* 7 and is equally important in the Aristotle's formulation of numerical and functional relatives in *Metaphysics* V.15. Reciprocity forms the basis of Aristotle's treatment of ratios, and because relations involving functional relatives are convertible (e.g., what can heat is relative to what can be heated, and what can be heated is relative to what can heat), those relatives exhibit a reciprocity as well. However, Aristotle's treatment of intentional relatives in *Metaphysics* V.15 shows that some relatives do not reciprocate. Thus, unlike in *Categories* 7, Aristotle does not here propose that every relative must have a reciprocating correlative.

Furthermore, Aristotle shows no serious concern for having to present an argument explicitly excluding substance from the category, an understandable omission given the theme and purpose of the *Metaphysics* as a whole, and perhaps his feeling of having already settled the matter (*Categories* 8b20). It is enough for him to note at *Metaphysics* 1021b8-11 that substances are only accidentally relatives. Later, at *Metaphysics* XIV, he reiterates that the relative is least of all things a real, concrete thing or substance. He argues that because there is no proper change, i.e., no generation, destruction or movement, with relational being it cannot be neither potentially or actually a substance (*Metaphysics* 1088a29). A relative can remain the same and at once be larger or less or equal depending upon that to which the relative is being compared (*Metaphysics* 1088a33-35).

Aristotle also omits discussion of various sorts of relatives from his *Metaphysics* account that he mentions in the *Categories* account. As Morales 1994, 267 notes, Aristotle omits spatial relations. Aristotle also neglects to mention such relatives as master and slave. Morales suggests that slave and master might fall under this class because something might *cause* a man to be a master (Morales 1994, 268). For instance, he might inherit his slaves from his father, or win them as the spoils of war.

Aristotle also seems to treat some kinds of relatives differently from before. He does not treat comparative relatives, for instance, at least not in the same way he does in *Categories* 7. In a sense *exceeding* and *exceeded* are comparatives in a way that *larger* and *smaller* are. We know that something has been exceeded by comparing the length, say, of one item against the length of the other item. In the same way, we determine whether something is larger or smaller than some thing. But there the similarity stops. Aristotle thinks that the *Categories* 7 comparatives, e.g., *larger* and *more beautiful*, are larger or more beautiful than some specific thing which is smaller or less beautiful. Although Aristotle calls all four relatives (the exceeding, the exceeded, the larger, and the more beautiful), he allows the first two to be "wholly indefinite." Indeed, Aristotle's inclusion of indefinite numerical relations into the category of relation is a significant difference between the two texts. One problem Aristotle leaves us, then, is that of reconciling, if we can, his inclusion of indefinite numerical relations in the *Metaphysics* with the knowing definitely criterion of *Categories* 7.

In *Categories* 7, we have seen that Aristotle mostly discusses relatives—the entities that qualify for inclusion within the category of relation. But at *Metaphysics* V 15, 1021b6-8, as Ackrill (1963, 98) notes, Aristotle speaks clearly of relations such as equality and similarity, according to which the things possessing them in pairs are called relata, e.g., equals and similars, even though Aristotle sticks to the same word *pros ti*, but clearly in a different sense, and does not introduce a new word for "relation".

We are by now familiar with Aristotle's basic intuition about relation. We have seen it in the *Categories* with his L and E accounts of relatives; we observed it in *Metaphysics* with his classifications of relatives and relations: Relational being always involves one thing being in relationship to another thing. And so despite the above differences I have pointed out between these two texts, Aristotle maintains the same regard for the dyadic nature of relational being. We are still left wondering, though, exactly what these relatives are that are in relationship to each other, what it means to know them definitely, and how best to understand the nature of the relationship between them. The investigation of these issues is what I take up next in Part Two.

Part One: The Problems and Solutions

Chapter 4

Interpreting Aristotle's Relatives

4. Introduction

In Chapter 4 I turn to the task of determining exactly what Aristotle's relatives are, i.e., the task of ascertaining their meta-ontological status. I will do this by focusing on Aristotle's *Categories* 7 accounts of relational being. Recall that in *Categories* 7, Aristotle presents two accounts of relational being. In the first account, *L*, Aristotle presents the basic characteristics or marks that allow a thing to be included in the category of relation. Some of the marks, for example, are that every relative must have its correlative, that relatives and correlatives are reciprocal, that most relatives have contraries, and so forth. But *L* also presents *linguistic* criteria for recognizing what is or is not a relative. Aristotle says that something is a relative when it is said to be *of* or *than* something else or is in some other way said to be relative to another thing (*Categories* 6a36–37, 6b6–8). Thus, we have Aristotle's initial view that a thing is a relative based on how it is *called* or *conceived of* (*legetai*).

The problem with L is that just about anything can satisfy the linguistic criterion of being called or said *of* something. For instance, merely being called *of* something else—say, the cow *of* Mrs. O'Leary or the hand *of* a person—is enough to qualify that thing as a relational entity. Since in Aristotle's meta-ontology substance is absolutely ontologically distinct from the other predicaments, his concern at *Categories* 8a13 is that some parts of secondary substances, for example, heads or hands, seem to be relatives by virtue of their meeting the L criterion for relational being. Aristotle offers E, his revised account of relatives, in an attempt to exclude from the category of relation those entities that he believes should be excluded, foremost of which is substance.

The E account of relational being moves away from the linguistic concerns of L and incorporates what I described in Chapter 2 as more metaphysical concerns. With E Aristotle is able to assure that substance is not a relative by giving a new formula of relational being that isolates features solely emblematic of the category of relation alone. I suggested in Chapter 2 that E comprises two key components. The first component is the "being" (*to einai*) component which brings a metaphysical character to the account by highlighting what is representative of relational being when no consideration whatsoever is given to substance.

I coined the second component the "holding somehow" *(pros ti pōs echein)* component. This second component spotlights Aristotle's special way of explaining what constitutes genuine relational being or what I have called "relationality". The "holding somehow" component specifies that being genuinely relational entails a holding somehow of one thing toward another thing. In Chapter 2 I offered some reasons why it seems reasonable to view the "holding somehow" component as supplying evidence that Aristotle does understand relation as being fundamentally dyadic in nature. I say more in Chapter 4 about why I think this is so.

Together, the being and holding somehow components allow Aristotle to give the revised account of relational being which says, in short, that being for a relative means for it to hold in some way toward another thing. But even with the revised account in hand, it is not easy to say precisely which one, or if more than one, of the types of relational entities Aristotle either alludes to or directly discusses in *Categories* 7 exemplifies a genuine relative entity. As I will show in Chapter 4, Aristotle seems to have numerous relational entities in mind throughout the text including (a) relative words (e.g., 'slave', 'double', 'larger'), (b) concrete relative items (e.g., the slave Peggy, a bowl of ice cream that is the double of a bowl with half as much ice cream, the mountain that is larger than another mountain) (c) metaphysical relational predicates (e.g., slave, double, larger), (d) relational attributes (or properties) (e.g., being a slave, being double, being larger), (e) relations (e.g., is a slave of, is double of, is larger than).

Below I examine interpretations of Aristotle's accounts of relatives given by three commentators: Ackrill (1963), Mignucci (1986), and Morales (1994). In each case I note the commentator's general interpretation of what kind of relational entity he thinks Aristotle has in mind as representative of genuine relative entities and what each sees as the significant feature or features of relatives. Next, I point out difficulties with the commentators' accounts and then I offer my own interpretation of Aristotle's relatives.

4.1 Ackrill's Interpretation of Relatives

Ackrill (1963, 75) contends that Aristotle's main preoccupation in the *Categories* is with things, not predicates or names. Ackrill states that it is "important to recognize from the start that the *Categories* is not primarily or explicitly about names, but about the things that names signify" (Ackrill 1963, 71). I would restate Ackrill's comment and say that the *Categories* is primarily about things as signified by names or about things as they present themselves for consideration and naming. While Ackrill states that the "*Categories* classify things, not words" (73), he believes that in *Categories* 7 Aristotle discusses the things that are relatives, i.e., the slave or the double, by describing relational predicates and occasionally relations themselves.

> In [*Categories* 7 Aristotle] does not, for the most part, treat of relations (similarity, slavery) but rather, in effect, of relational predicates ('similar', 'slave'). (Ackrill 1963, 98)

Ackrill says, however, that Aristotle

> does not put the matter in this linguistic way. He does not say that 'larger' and 'slave' are relatives, but that the larger and the slave are relatives. However, he does not, of course, mean that, for example, the slave Callias is a relative (he is a substance), but that Callias is a relative in so far as he is *called a slave*; in other words, 'slave' is a relative term. (Ackrill 1963, 98; italics Ackrill)

There are several things here to point out right away. First, when Ackrill says that Aristotle is discussing "relational predicates", Ackrill must mean either relational words or what I am calling grammatical relational predicates as opposed to metaphysical predicates. This would seem clear from Ackrill's caveat that Aristotle himself does not "put the matter in this *linguistic* way" (Italics mine). This reading is further supported by the distinction Ackrill 1963 attempts to draw a few sentences later when he says that Aristotle

> (1)   does not say that 'larger' and 'slave' are relatives, but that the larger and the slave are relatives. (98)

The point Ackrill is driving at in (1) is that he believes Aristotle thinks a thing that is larger (i.e., a concrete item that is larger than something) is a relative, not that the word 'larger' is a relative.

Ackrill tries to clarify this distinction further.

> (2)   However, [Aristotle] does not, of course, mean that, for example, the slave Callias is a relative (he is a substance), but that Callias is a relative in so far as he is *called a slave*; in other words, 'slave' is a relative term. (Ackrill 1963, 98, italics Ackrill)

While Ackrill does make the general distinction clear between considering something a relational word or a relational concrete item, he fails to put the matter correctly when he tries to explain why

> (3)   Callias is a relative in so far as he is *called a slave*

but that

> (4)   the slave Callias

is not a relative. Now, what Ackrill means is that without further qualification, (4) simply refers to a primary substance; namely,

> (5)   Callias

Because Aristotle has said that no substance is a relative, Ackrill thinks that Aristotle regards neither (4) nor (5) as relatives. But what Ackrill fails to make clear is that (3) is no less a substance than either (4) or (5) because (3), (4), and (5) all in some way represent concrete items.

With respect to relatives, Ackrill suggests that what Aristotle takes to be a categorical relative is a concrete thing given under a relational description. The point Ackrill wants to make, even if he puts it somewhat poorly, is that certain things are called relative because they have properties that are relative. As Ackrill 1963, 98 notes, Aristotle makes this distinction clear at *Metaphysics* 1021b6–8:

> Further, there are properties in virtue of which the things that have them are called relatives, e.g., equality is relative because the equal is, and likeness because the like is. (trans. Ross)

Second, note that Ackrill regards sentence fragments that contain relative words to be *incomplete*. Ackrill gives

(6) 'Callias is larger'

as an example of an incomplete statement (Ackrill 1963, 98–99). A sentence fragment is incomplete if the fragment needs to be completed by some other expression or expressions in order to form a complete sentence. While the context may allow 'Callias is larger' to be intelligible, we need to know with regard to whom, or to what, Callias is larger for the statement to be complete. That is, some correlative needs to be stated.

Thus Ackrill disagrees with Aristotle with regard to (7):

(7) Callias is a slave

Ackrill believes (7) has a complete enough meaning not to require the addition of the correlative word 'master'. What (7) reveals, Ackrill says, is not an incompleteness, but an *indefiniteness*. For Ackrill, (7) is

> perfectly intelligible without knowledge of the context, though it has a certain indefiniteness; it is equivalent to 'Callias is the slave *of someone*'. (Ackrill 1963, 99; italics Ackrill)

I think Ackrill is incorrect here, for although we may consider slave to have a complete sense, it is clear that Aristotle does not. The thrust of both *L* and *E* is that being a relative means being somehow related to something. In my view, we should take seriously the "holding someway" component of *E*, and not just the general way in which relatives are thought of as being *of* something. By taking care to do this, the relationship between the relative and the correlative becomes apparent. For example, in the case of <u>slave</u>, let us say that the "holding somehow" component of E entails that:

> (8)   Being a slave is the same as being a human being owned by another human being.

What (8) says is that to be a slave is to be owned by someone. If this is so, then the statement:

> (9)   Callias is a slave

will be equivalent to:

> (10)   Callias is owned by _____

In Aristotle's view, (9) needs completion just as much as (10) and so cannot be considered "complete".

Ackrill 1963 mentions what he calls four "undeniable" facts about the two accounts of relatives Aristotle gives at *Categories* 7, accounts I have labeled L and E.[21] Ackrill says that

> (a) according to Aristotle [the L criterion] makes heads and hands relatives while the [E criterion] does not;
>
> (b) the [L criterion] refers to what is *said*, what things are *called*, while the second does not (hence the traditional terms *secundum dici* and *secundum esse*;
>
> (c) Aristotle says that whatever satisfies the [E criterion] also satisfies the first (8a33)
>
> (d) the [E criterion] is said to have a consequence concerning the necessity of 'knowing definitely' that to which something is related (8a35-37), and the fact that this necessity does not hold in the case of heads and hands is taken to show that they are not, by the revised criterion, relatives (8b15-19). (Ackrill 1963, 101-102, italics Ackrill)

Other than the above, Ackrill gives no direct analysis of E but looks to the knowing definitely criterion to distinguish further L from E.

4.2 Mignucci's Interpretation of Relatives

In many respects Mignucci's (1986) interpretation is at odds with Ackrill's. First, although Mignucci admits that Aristotle sometimes speaks as though he is interested in the objects that possess relational properties, Mignucci flatly rejects Ackrill's view that Aristotle's relatives are things under relational description.

> One might think that what has to be counted as a relative is the mountain: it is the mountain that is what it is, i.e., large, with respect to something else. But I do not believe that Aristotle would have considered a mountain to be in the category of the relatives nor does it make any sense to say that a mountain is a relative *qua* large. What is meant to be a relative is the property of being large. (Mignucci 1986, 103)

For Mignucci, to say that the mountain *qua* large is relative is the same as inferring that the mountain itself is a relative because it is large. Mignucci 1986, 102 suggests let 'F' be "large", 'G' be "a relative", and '*a*' be "mountain." He contends that:

(11)   *a qua* F is G

is equivalent to saying that:

(12)   *a* is G because it is F

What we have done, he says, is to infer:

(13)   *a* is G

from

(14)   *a* is F

Now (13) says that the mountain is a relative, but since Aristotle excludes primary substance from the category, the mountain cannot be a relative. Rather, "what is meant to be a relative," Mignucci says, "is the property of being large" (103).

> If this interpretation is adopted, terms such as τὸ μεῖζον and τὸ διπλάσιον . . . or . . . τὸ ὅμοιον do not refer to things which are larger or double or

similar, but stand for the predicates or the properties larger, double, similar. When Aristotle says that larger is said to be larger with respect to something, he means the "larger" in its use implies a reference to something else. (Mignucci 1986, 203)

Mignucci 1986, 101 characterizes L^{22} as Aristotle's first definition of what it means to be a relational property. I agree with him that Aristotle's comments technically cannot be called a definition. Although Mignucci never suggests that a relative is a relation, he does consider a relative to be a relational property that entails a relation, the terms of which are determined *intensionally* in that the terms are determined by the sense or meaning of the property in question (105–106). As Mignucci puts it, "there must be a reference to a specified relation that alone or together with other properties characterizes the relative at issue" (Mignucci 1986, 105). Mignucci holds, therefore, that an L relative is actually an L-relational property. Mignucci takes

Aristotle's definition of relatives to mean exactly that a property F is said to be a relative property if, and only if, it can be expanded into a relation that determines F univocally. (Mignucci 1986, 104).

That is, for F to be a relative property, it must have a relation entailed within it that is capable of specifying F precisely. He gives the following as an example of a formal expression for such L-relational properties (Mignucci 1986, 104–105):

(15) $\lambda x F(x) = \lambda x \exists y R_F(x,y)$[23]

(15) consists of a relational property and its constitutive relation. These two parts of (15) are identified as follows: '$\lambda x F(x)$' is a lambda class indicator that represents a relational property, and '$\lambda x \exists y R_F(x,y)$' represents the relation that is entailed in, i.e., is constitutive of, that property. For Mignucci, "the relation $\lambda x \exists y R_F(x,y)$ which is used for defining the relational property $\lambda x F(x)$ is a well determined relation whose choice depends intrinsically on F" (Mignucci 1986, 105).

Each of the smaller components of (15) are analyzable as follows: The lambda class indicator includes the lambda operator, 'λ', which signifies class inclusion; the predicate '$F(x)$' stands for an L-relational property and is read "x has F" or "x is an F". Taken together, the lambda class indicator reads: "the class of all things x which have the property F" or "the class of all things x which satisfy $F(x)$". Next, the identity sign, '=', indicates that the expressions on either side of the sign are equivalent; the existential quantifier, '∃y', represents the existence of some individual; and last, the relational predicate, '$R_F(x,y)$', which is read "x has an F-relation to y."

And so we read (15) as:

(15*) For the class of all x which satisfy $F(x)$ there exists a y such that x bears an F-relation to y.

Under Mignucci's reading of L, then, the L relative <u>slave</u> stands for a relational property, <u>being a slave</u> that contains a reference to a relation that characterizes the relative, <u>slave</u>.

From (15*), we now can give the domain of the relation entailed in the relational property of <u>being a slave</u>:

(16) The class of all individuals that have the property of being a slave, is such that for individuals in this class, there exists another individual, y, such that individuals having the property of being a slave bear an is <u>a slave of</u> relation to that y.

We can restate (16) more plainly by supposing once again that what it means to be a slave is to be a human being owned by a human being. Let 'S' be the L-relational property <u>being a slave</u>. Following this interpretation (Mignucci 1986, 105–106), when S is predicated of Peggy, there is a relation, $\lambda x\exists yR_S(x,y)$, entailed in predicating the property $\lambda xS(x)$ of Peggy. Since the connection between the property and the relation is due to the meaning of the property, saying that Peggy has the property of being a slave amounts to saying that:

(17) Peggy has the property of being owned by someone and that someone exists.

With respect to the *aporia* about including substance in the category of relation, Mignucci remarks that Aristotle sees a clear need to revise L:

a condition must be given which allows us to isolate a subclass of the class of [L relatives] in which the parts of secondary substances are not contained (*Cat.* 7, 8a33-35). It follows immediately from this way of putting things that [E relatives] are conceived of as a proper subclass of L-relatives: every L relative is also [an E relative], but there are [L relatives] which are not [E relatives]. (Mignucci 1986, 106)

Mignucci thinks that since all relatives that are E-relative are also L-relative, the lambda class indicator, $\lambda x F(x)$, of (17) may also be used to symbolize an E-relational property (Mignucci 1986, 106, 110).

As for the kind of relation Aristotle's E formulation represents, I concur with Mignucci that E cannot be a formula for internal relations (Mignucci 1986, 107). A relation R is internal if and only if, for all x, x's relation to y by R is an essential property of x. *Metaphysics* 1035b10-25 indicates that Aristotle thinks it is an essential property of a human head for it to be the functioning head of a human being. If this is an essential property of a human head, then a functioning human head must be something internally related to a human being. But if E is an account of internal relations, and such things as heads and hands are internally related to the human body, then E would allow inclusion into the category of relation of the very things the formula was meant to exclude.

Mignucci finds the meaning of the scholastic classification relatives *secundum dici* and *secundum esse* difficult to ascertain, and rejects this scholastic method of distinguishing L relatives from E relatives (Mignucci 1986, 107). Likewise, he finds the meaning of Greek word *einai* ("being"), in what I have called the being component of E (*Categories* 8a31–33), "far from clear" (108).

While I certainly agree with Mignucci that the text at *Categories* 8a31–33 is not as transparently clear as one would like, I disagree entirely that "without further information from Aristotle it is *useless* to try to solve the problem" of interpreting E. (Italics mine) Even my preliminary discussion of E and its components provides, I think, a useful means to interpret E and offers insight into how Aristotle conceives of the categorical formulation of relational being.

I also disagree that the *secundum dici-secundum esse* distinction is so obscure as to preclude its usefulness in articulating the distinction between L and E. Recall that L must be amended precisely because some relatives that count as relatives only due to their linguistic features would not be considered relatives on the basis of their meta-ontological features. Aristotle clearly was aware of the difference between linguistic and ontological modes of analysis and their respective limitations. I believe he attempts to mark the different relational status of L and E relatives by his use of *legetai* formula for the one and *einai* formula (or more exactly, the *to einai tō pros ti pōs echein* formula) for the other. Without offering further support for my position, I will simply say that I think the *secundum dici-secundum esse* distinction does mark the difference Aristotle draws between a thing's meeting a linguistic, as opposed to a meta-ontological, standard of relationality. In any event, Mignucci eschews further examination of *E* and, as Ackrill did, looks to the knowing definitely criterion to differentiate Aristotle's two accounts of relational being.

4.3 Morales's Interpretation of Relatives

Morales's (1994) commentary closely parallels that of Ackrill (1963) and Mignucci (1986) while diverging in some respects from both. For example, Morales agrees with Ackrill that "in the *Categories* [Aristotle] is classifying entities, not predicates" (Morales 1994, 261). However, Morales believes that Aristotle nonetheless relies on the meaning of relational terms as an orientation for the classification of relatives.

> Now, although it seems clear that the *Categories* deal with entities, not with words or concepts, most of the time Aristotle does recur, as an orientation for his classification, to the linguistic meaning of the terms involved. (Morales 1994, 260)

He agrees with Mignucci 1986, 106 that the linguistic meaning of relative words is an aid in determining what the proper correlative of a relative should be, i.e., the "*meaning* of the term has to be considered in order to determine if a relative exists or not" (Morales 1994, 261; italics Morales). Morales says that "it is the relational term's meaning which tell us what to look for in eventual correlates" (263).

But unlike Mignucci, Morales agrees with Ackrill that when Aristotle speaks of "the slave," he means the concrete item insofar as it possesses the attribute of being a slave, or as Morales puts it, insofar as it possesses the relational predicate slave.

> Since he lays emphasis on the "things related", and not on the relation itself, he uses the technical expression τὰ πρός τί "things [said] in relation to [something else]", in order to address what we might call the "correlates" or "relata" of a relation... But he addresses these relata *in so far* as they possess relational predicates. Instead of speaking of abstract relations like "slavery" or "equality", he mentions "the slave" and "the equal". (Morales 1994, 256; italics Morales)

Morales thinks that for Aristotle "all true relatives are concrete instances of relatives" (263) and that, for Aristotle a relative generally implies the existence of (at least two underlying things (subject and object) that stand in the corresponding relation. (Morales 1994, 261)

From Morales's perspective, then, Aristotle considers genuine relatives to be concrete relatives, i.e., the actual items that stand in relation to each other, and that Aristotle discusses concrete relatives, i.e., the *relata* and *correlates* of a relation, by means of relational words.

Morales considers L^{24} Aristotle's attempt to classify as relatives those attributes whose true predication implies three things: (a) the existence of the relative's subject or ontological ground, (b) the existence of the correlate, and (c) that there may be a grammatically correct way to express the concrete relation's correlate.

Therefore, according to [Aristotle's first definition, *L*], the term slave", when truly predicated, entails: 1) the existence of the subject, e.g., Callias, 2) the existence of the correlate, i.e., a given master, and 3) the possibility of eliciting the concrete relation by mentioning the correlate in the appropriate grammatical case. (Morales 1994, 261)

Here Morales mirrors Mignucci's view that the true predication of a relative implies the existence of an actual relation (Mignucci 1986, 104–105).

Overall, I think that thus far Morales's interpretation is correct. We know Aristotle's ontology requires that an accident be dependent on its subject and that this ontological dependence pertains to both the relative and its correlative since both the relative and correlative must have their grounds. So, at the very least, if Aristotle wants to insist that every relative has its correlative (*Categories* 6b28), then he must think that the true predication of a relational attribute of its subject implies the existence of the correlative's subject.

I disagree, however, with Morales's position that a relative word "can (but does not have to) be mentioned in the appropriate grammatical case" (Morales 1994, 260–261). This would make it seem as though the linguistic demands of *L* were optional. Morales follows Ackrill 1963, 99 in thinking that certain genera of relatives which Aristotle names are not in fact relational entities:

Nor do the words "state", "condition", "knowledge" and "perception" have to be followed in Greek by the genitive case, but they are nevertheless presented by Aristotle (6b2 f.) as instances of relational entities. (Morales 1994, 259)

As I mentioned in Chapter 2, alternative translations of *hexis* (i.e., "possession" or "habit") and *diathesis* (i.e., "disposition") for Ackrill's "state" and "condition" would reflect *L*'s prepositional requirement that relatives generally use "*of*" or "*toward*" to introduce their correlative objects. By using "possession" and "disposition", for example, the objects they intend might have been more obvious: A science or a virtue is a *possession* of a field of objects, i.e., things to be known or right things to be done (see above p. 47).

Furthermore, Aristotle makes it clear that new words be coined in order to make the correlativity of the relatives apparent (*Categories* 7a18–19). If the linguistic criteria of *L* were not important, Aristotle would not have suggested that we go to such lengths to meet *L*'s criteria. This suggests that Aristotle considers the linguistic requirements of *L* as necessary, not optional.

Morales briefly acknowledges that what I have called the "being" (*to einai*) component of *E* points to a thing's categorical status. After explaining why the parts of substance do not meet *E*, Morales concludes by saying that

> their "being" (τό εἶναι, 8a32)—and that means in this context: their categorical status—is *not* "the same as being somehow related to something." (Morales 1994, 266; italics Morales)

But Morales mostly addresses the being component of *E* in strictly existential terms. He focuses on the existence of concrete relatives and the way in which the knowing definitely criterion, which Aristotle considers to be a consequence of *E* (*Categories* 8a36), points to the necessary and sufficient conditions for a relative to exist (Morales 1994, 263, 266). One necessary condition for a relative to exist is the existence of the underlying subject of both the relative and its correlative.

> Now, since for Aristotle all true relatives are concrete instances of relatives, then, in order to ascertain if a relative *exists*, one has to examine not only the subject to which the relative is supposed to apply, but also the things with which this subject is supposed to relate: for the purpose of determining if a man is a "slave", or a number a "double", one has to examine the way in which the man or the number in question is related *to other things*. And the other way round: if we know with certainty that a slave or a double exists, then we know by the same token that some corresponding master or half exists. (Morales 1994, 263; italics Morales)

Morales correctly asserts that the existence of the relatum and correlate are entailed in actual relations. In his view the existence of a concrete relative "implies the existence of (at least two) underlying things (subject and object) that stand in the corresponding relation" (Morales 1994, 261). He acknowledges that, excepting intentional relatives, actual existing relatives cannot be conceived of or realized without a reference to their simultaneously existing correlatives. Morales does not examine in any great detail what I have called the holding somehow component of E, but he does notice one key aspect of it when he states that "one has to examine the *way* in which the man or the number in question is related to other things" (Morales 1994, 263; italics mine).

Lastly, Morales thinks the *secundum dici-secundum esse* distinction may characterizes the difference between L and E.

> While the criterion contained in [L] seems to refer to what is *said*, what things are *called* (*secundum dici*), the one contained in [E] apparently has to do with what things *are* (*secundum esse*). It has consequently been noticed that the first criterion is linguistic, whereas the second is ontological. (Morales 1994, 260; italics Morales)

Morales does not directly examine E further, except to say, as Ackrill and Mignucci have, that the knowing definitely criterion helps further distinguish L from E. In Chapter 5 I will discuss more fully Morales's views about the knowing definitely criterion and its integral relationship with E, but for now I want to examine a difficulty with Morales's interpretation of indefiniteness that affects his general analysis of Aristotle's relatives.

Morales places great stress on what he regards as the principal feature of a relative: its indefiniteness (or "incompleteness" as Ackrill puts it). He says that he

> will try to show that Aristotle's criterion for recognizing relational attributes is based on their peculiar *indefiniteness*. This indefiniteness may be eliminated by a 'definite knowledge'—and the eventual specification—of the correlate in the specific instance of the relation. (Morales 1994, 261)

What I find problematic is Morales's notion that the indefiniteness of relational attributes may be eliminated by a definite knowledge.

The first thing to notice is that although Morales's commentary closely follows Ackrill's commentary of *Categories* 7, he does not mean the same thing Ackrill does when Ackrill claims that relative words (e.g., 'slave') are indefinite. What Ackrill calls "incomplete" Morales calls "indefinite". Recall that Ackrill considers statements with relative words incomplete because in order for the statements to have a complete sense they require some other word. When we use the word 'smaller', e.g., in the statement fragment

(18) Pasadena is smaller than _____

we must mention what it is Pasadena is smaller than in order for the statement to form a complete sentence as in (19):

(19) Pasadena is smaller than Dallas.

For Ackrill, 'indefinite' refers to relative words that for him are not entirely incomplete, such as 'slave' (Ackrill 1963, 99). For Morales, on the other hand, 'indefinite' means "entirely incomplete". Morales states that relational predicates (e.g., "is similar to", "is double of") are indefinite and have to be "supplemented by the mention of the intended correlates before they can build true or false sentences" (Morales 1994, 261). That is, we must add to (18) mention of the correlate to make a true sentence such as (19) or false one such as (20):

(20) Pasadena is smaller than Claremont.

Morales agrees with Ackrill that some relatives, e.g., slave, are not as indefinite (or "incomplete" as Ackrill would say) as other relational entities. Because slave has a "comparatively complete sense," Morales says, it is less definite. He believes that other relational words do not have such a comparatively complete sense because they are "too vague" not to mention their correlatives. But even in cases such as slave where the context may allow for the correlative to remain unmentioned, Morales says we nevertheless understand that the slave stands in relation to some other item.

> The fact that some relational terms like "slave" . . . are endowed with a comparatively complete sense does not mean that they do not satisfy [*L*]; it means that in ordinary language we often denote or qualify things by alluding to a relation in which they stand to something else, without mentioning explicitly the latter (we do not estimate this relevant in some contexts). For instance, we say "Callias, the slave", or "Callias *is* a slave". Still, even in these cases, we do assume that the denoted (or qualified) things stand in particular relations to *other*

things. The reason "the double" or "the greater" do not possess this comparatively "complete sense" is that they are much to vague to be used this way. (Morales 1994, 261; italics Morales)

Whether we call it incompleteness or indefiniteness, I agree with Ackrill and Morales that the key feature of relational being, as Aristotle sees it, is a relative's need to be complemented by reference to some other item. Thus, Morales's use of "indefinite" as a descriptor of this need is not worrisome in and of itself.

What is worrisome is Morales's peculiar notion that the indefiniteness of the relative

may be eliminated by a 'definite knowledge'—and the eventual specification—of the correlate in the specific instance of the relation. (Morales 1994, 261)

Morales sometimes speaks, as above, about the way in which relatives are eliminated by the specification of the correlative or correlate. Elsewhere he speaks of the indefiniteness of the relative being "corrected" once the relational predicate is supplemented by mention of the appropriate correlative.

[I]f the predicates contain relational terms, their indefiniteness may be *corrected* by mentioning the correlate. (Morales 1994, 262; italics mine)

What does Morales mean by such talk of relatives being eliminated or corrected by mention of the correlate? Let me take up the latter notion first.

Morales introduces the idea that the indefiniteness of relational predicates may be corrected in a passage where he discusses the law of non-contradiction (Morales 1994, 262). The law of non-contradiction states that one cannot simultaneously predicate contrary attributes of the same subject, in the same respect, at the same time. Socrates cannot be both tall and short at the same time and in the same respect and in relation to the same individual.

By saying that a relational predicate may be corrected by mention of the correlate, perhaps Morales is thinking that the potential for contradiction is a deficiency, and that this deficiency is corrected when grammatical relational predicates such as '. . . is shorter than _____' are completed with appropriate words. Thus, when we say

(21)   Socrates is shorter than Simmias

and

(22)   Socrates is taller Xantippe

we do not violate the law of non-contradiction because, on Aristotle's account, it is clear in respect to what Socrates is both taller and shorter than (see *Metaphysics* 1005b12-20).

On the other hand, Morales's use of "corrected" may be closer to his use of "eliminated" in the passage quoted earlier in which he states that the relative's "indefiniteness may be eliminated by a 'definite knowledge'—and the eventual specification—of the correlate in the specific instance of the relation" (Morales 1994, 261). From this passage we see Morales making a direct connection between the items actually involved in a specific relation, e.g., 'Peggy' and 'Tucker' or 'the double' and 'the half', and what he thinks it takes to satisfy the knowing definitely criterion. On his view, it is the definite knowledge of the correlates of the actual relation that eliminates the indefiniteness.

Now, as to Morales's notion that the indefiniteness of a relative may be eliminated, Morales appears to associate this with the logical sense of "satisfied". This becomes evident when he describes how the blanks of a grammatical relational predicate are filled by appropriate terms. In Morales's initial discussion of *L*, he remarks that

> [Aristotle] seems to be to be talking about terms such as "larger", "double', etc., which correspond to relational predicates ("is larger than", "is double of") containing at least two free variables (subject and one or more objects) which have to be satisfied before the predicate can provide a complete sentence. (Morales 1994, 258)

What with talk of "variables" being "satisfied" before the "predicate can provide a complete sentence," it is not entirely clear whether Morales is talking about grammatical relational predicates or logical ones since one may speak both of them forming complete sentences. His use of "variable" suggests a logical analysis; the mention of "a complete sentence" suggests a grammatical one. Nevertheless, the Morales's view of relatives being eliminated and corrected falls in line with his notion of the free variables of relational predicates being satisfied. For in one case the indefiniteness of the relatives is eliminated by mention of the appropriate correlative item and in the other the relational predicate is corrected by mention of one or both members of the appropriate pair of relative and correlative items. In each case Morales considers the appropriate mention of the correlative (or relative and correlative pair) as something that eliminates, corrects, or satisfies the indefiniteness of the relative.

Lastly, besides stating that relatives may be eliminated or corrected, Morales also contends that some relatives "cease to be" once they have been determined. Now when Morales speaks of a relative's being determined he appears to have two things in mind. First, he thinks of a relative being determined when its correlative is mentioned. As I just noted, in Morales's view this specification of the appropriate correlative removes the indefiniteness of the relational predicate.

Second, there is the sense that one term determines the other when it helps to specify or mark out the other's definition or content. Let me attempt to reconstruct the point Morales is making. At this juncture, at the end of Morales's commentary on *Categories* 7, he has just returned to an examination of *E* and is offering further reasons why the parts of substance fail to meet *E*. In Chapter 5 I discuss Morales's analysis of the *aporia* concerning substance being a relative, so I will not embark on any detailed comment about it here, save this synopsis.

Morales argues that heads and hands do not count as relatives because they are too complete; they are not indefinite enough to qualify as relatives. Their definiteness is evident, he says, from their definitions. For instance, the definition of hand, he maintains, already contains within it a reference to the whole, i.e., as being a part of the body. Morales suggests that the asymmetrical relationship the parts of substance have to their wholes is not unlike the asymmetrical relationship intentional relatives and correlatives have with each other. With respect to the third class of relatives Aristotle mentions at *Metaphysics* V.15, Morales explains that these intentional relational entities (e.g., the knowable, the thinkable) exhibit a logical priority in that

> in some pairs of relational attributes one of the relata may be used to determine the other. For example, the knowable (i.e., the object of knowledge), being prior to knowledge, gives knowledge its specific content and may be used to define it: grammar may be defined as (a kind of) "knowledge of letters", or music as (a kind of) "knowledge of sounds". (Morales 1994, 269)

Hence, due to the logical priority of the relative, an asymmetrical relationship exists between it and its correlative such that the relative defines or determines its correlative.

We now have a good idea what Morales means by a relative's being determined. Next we must see why he thinks some relatives "cease to be" once their determination takes place. Morales notes that Aristotle puts the genus knowledge in the category of relation but places a species of knowledge, grammar, outside the category of relation (Morales 1994, 265). The reason knowledge qualifies as a relative is because it is, in Morales's terminology, indefinite: knowledge is always knowledge *of* something. However, once we specify a particular kind of knowledge, for example, the knowledge of grammar, we find that grammar itself is not relative because grammar is not grammar *of* something (see *Categories* 11a24–31). The difficulties with Aristotle's placing a species outside the category of its genus need not concern us here.[25] The point Morales wants to make is that the indefiniteness of knowledge is eliminated once it is determined by mention of its species, grammar.

We are now ready to see the connection Morales wants to make between the notion of relatives being determined and of intentional relatives ceasing to be once their determination takes place. Morales concludes his remarks about the parts of substance not being *E*-relative by contending that with

> "the part and the whole", the relata have an asymmetrical way of referring to each other: the part is defined by reference to the whole (as fulfilling a particular function in it), but the whole is not defined by reference to the part. Since relatives of the third groups may cease to be such once their determination has taken place, the parts of substances (like hand, head, etc.) do not really belong to the category of the relative. (Morales 1994, 270).

Here is what I take Morales to mean: Once the knowable has been precisely determined as grammar, for example, what was once a relative entity (i.e., the knowable) ceases to be a relative entity and becomes a non-relational entity (i.e., grammar). This is at least one sense, then, in which Morales thinks a relative may cease to be a relative once its determination has taken place.

This idea of a relative being determined, and more specifically, of a relational genus being determined such that it no longer is a relational entity, leads Morales to introduce a worry for which he claims to have no real solution:

> It may perhaps be objected that if a relational genus can be so determined that it turns into a non-relational item, then this possibility

should be granted to all relatives. In this way, every relational predicate would have a chance to be supplemented by means of the definite knowledge of its correlate and, once being thus "satisfied", turn into a non-relational predicate. (Morales 1994, 266)

Morales thinks that for Aristotle, just as knowledge is determined or defined by the knowable, the part (e.g., a hand) is determined or defined in reference to the whole. Since in certain cases the determination of a relational item (e.g., here a relational genus) can affect the categorial status of the relational partner (e.g., in this case its species), the worry arises that any relative-correlative pairing is vulnerable to same over-determination and elimination. Why? Because what completes every grammatical relational predicate is the specification of the predicate's relative and correlative terms. Having definite knowledge of these terms implies that they have been specified in some manner, and that the grammatical relational predicate's indefiniteness has thereby been eliminated. For Morales, without its indefiniteness, the predicate ceases to be a *relational* predicate.

To sum up, then, given Morales's interpretation one is left with the possibility that even though grammatical relational predicates (e.g., is larger than, is double of) and the relational words within those predicates are indefinite, when the predicates are completed with their correlates, the indefiniteness of the predicate is eliminated and the predicate's relational status is potentially undermined.

There is yet another worry Morales raises. Since on his view the appropriate correlate for relative-correlative pairs is identified through the meaning of the relative word, it appear that the correlative is already contained, as it were, in the relative. The relative would already be completed before any explicit reference is made to its correlative. Mignucci's interpretation of Aristotle's relatives as properties with constitutive relations would also be vulnerable to this difficulty, too. For what is entailed in the true predication of a relational property, on Mignucci's account, is just the constitutive relation that is already a entailed as part of that property (Mignucci 1986, 104-105).

All three of Morales's notions I have just examined (i.e., that relatives become corrected, eliminated, or cease to be once they become determined) reflect, to one degree or another, a serious misunderstanding of Aristotle's relational theory. Morales improperly puts Aristotle's demand—that relatives be known definitely—at odds with the indefiniteness (in Morales's words) required of all relational being. The two notions—the indefiniteness of relational being and the knowing definitely criterion—are connected, but not in the way Morales's interpretation suggests they are. Given Morales's insistence that indefiniteness is the hallmark of relatives, it is not surprising, then, that confusion arises when he discusses the completion of grammatical relational predicates and the instantiation of actual relations by the mention of specific relative items.

According to both *Categories* 7 and *Metaphysics* V.15, every relative must have its correlative, i.e., every relative must be complemented by its correlative whether that correlative is required to be a reciprocal correlative or not (see *Categories* 6a37 ff., *Categories* 6b28-31, *Topics* 142a28-31, and *Sophistical Refutations* 181b25-28). Let us call this the criteria of complementarity. This criteria of complementarity works hand in hand with the knowing definitely criterion. The knowing definitely criterion says that if one knows a relative definitely, one will also know definitely that in relation to which the relative is holding somehow (*Categories* 8a35-38). If it were not for the mandatory complementarity of relational being, there would be no need for the demand to know *both* the correlative and the relative.

Morales seems to think that once the relative has been determined by the specification of the correlate, the relative's indefiniteness is vitiated. That is, in Morales's view, the grammatical relational predicates are indefinite in both

(23)   '. . . is older than _____'

and

(24)   Leonytne is older than _____

but the indefiniteness is determined away, so to speak, in (27):

(25) Leonytne is older than Jessye.

Recall that for Morales, what one is to know definitely are the actual items standing in relation to each other, i.e., terms of an actual relation.

> Now, since for Aristotle all true relatives are concrete instances of relatives, then, in order to ascertain if a relative *exists*, one has to examine not only the subject to which the relative is supposed to apply, but also the things with which this subject is supposed to relate. (Morales 1994, 263; italics Morales)

What follows from this? If I understand Morales correctly, the fact of my having definite knowledge of Leontyne's being older than Jessye, and the filling in of both blanks of (23) and the one blank of (24), effectively eliminates the indefiniteness of the relational predicate older than in (25). What Morales's interpretation does not do is to affirm in (25) the complementarity of the relative older than or of Leonytne's being older than. Rather, it jeopardizes the relational status of (25). But this is an absurd outcome, for both (25) and the reality it represents are just the kind of thing Aristotle adduces as evidence of genuine relational being.

What of the idea Morales 1994, 270 posits that relatives "*cease to be*" once their determination has taken place? Morales's interpretation of indefiniteness hampers him to such an extent that his analysis cannot account for both the constitutive indefiniteness of relational being and at the same time account for the fact that all relatives must show evidence of complementarity such that in their existing, they hold somehow toward something. In short, his analysis winds up making the idea of knowing definitely the relative-correlative pair something antithetical to the necessary complementarity of relatives. In so doing, Morales badly misses the point of Aristotle's remarks and puts himself in the untenable position of having his remarks imply that once a relative actually is a relative—i.e., once the relatum and correlate do stand in relation to each other—the relative is no longer relational.

This is not what either *Categories* 7 or *Metaphysics* V.15 tells us. Rather, what we learn from *Categories* 7 is that when a relative is truly predicated of something, the resulting relata are indeed relational. If the terms—whatever we take a 'term' to be here, e.g., a concrete or linguistic item—were not relatives, they would not be understood to be holding somehow in relation to each other in accordance with *E*. Clearly with *E* and the knowing definitely criterion, Aristotle cannot be demanding that a relative have its relational complement (i.e., a correlative) while simultaneously maintaining that a relative's having such a complement destroys the relative's fundamental relationality.

I admit that the difference between Morales's and my own way of interpreting this feature is much like the difference between one person seeing a glass as half full and the other person seeing it as half empty. If we take Morales's comments to their logical conclusion, it means both the grammatical and logical relational predicate must remain permanently and wholly incomplete in order to preserve the requisite indefiniteness of relational being. On my view, however, Aristotle would not have us recognize relational being by its static gappiness, i.e., by its perpetual lack of a reference to some thing. Instead, an analysis of Aristotle's relatives must give appropriate weight to both the relative's required gappiness and its complementarity. Morales errs in overemphasizing the former to the detriment of the latter.

I would make a similar criticism of Morales's worry that all relatives might be considered semantically too complete to count as a relative. Relational pairs such as slave-master and double-half exhibit the mandatory complementarity Aristotle thinks each individual relative must have. But as Morales points out, these and other relational attributes may be thought of as intensionally conjoined because of their respective meanings. Since the relatives would in a sense already contain a reference to their correlative attribute, they would never be missing their relational complement. Hence, they would not be gappy enough to count as genuine relatives. In the end, though, I do not think the difficulty is as problematic as Morales supposes.

In the *Sophistical Refutations* Aristotle goes so far as to suggest that relative words are practically devoid of meaning without the mention of their correlatives. And if they do still retain some meaning, it is not the meaning they normally would have when a relative word is used in conjunction with its correlative.

> With respect to those who draw one into repeating the same thing a number of times, it is clear that one must not grant that predications of relative terms have any meaning in abstraction by themselves, e.g. double apart from double of half, purely on the ground that it figures in it. For 'ten' figures in ten minus one and 'do' in not do, and generally the affirmation in the negation; nevertheless, for all that, if someone says that this is not white, he does not say that it is white. Double, perhaps, has not even any meaning at all, any more than half; and even if it has a meaning, it has not the same meaning as in the combination. (*Sophistical Refutations* 181b25-34)

Aristotle makes the same point at *Topics* 142a28–31.

> However, one must look to see whether it is not possible to define some things in any other way, e.g. the double without the half, and all terms that are essentially relative; for in all such cases *to be them is the same as to be somehow related to something*, so that it is impossible to know the one without the other, and similarly in the account of the one the other must also be embraced.[26]

Both the *Sophistical Refutations* and *Topics* passages above show that Aristotle realizes that relative words have an interdependent semantic relationship. Aristotle is saying that an account of one relative word must include an account of its correlative. Since these words are defined in terms of each other, the one, in this sense, is contained in the other. The question is: Does this semantic interdependence diminish the incompleteness or indefiniteness of the relative word?

It is clear that Aristotle does not think so. The point Aristotle makes in both passages is precisely this: relative words are so incomplete that an account of a relative word cannot be given without reference to its correlative expression. All the texts under consideration (*Categories* 7, *Metaphysics* V.15, and those above) suggest that semantic interdependency does not eliminate the indefiniteness of relative words. Once again, I think the worry Morales raises stems from his over-emphasis on what I have called his "perpetual" indefiniteness view of relational being. Aristotle would say the kind of indefiniteness Morales is looking for is, from a semantic viewpoint at least, hardly possible and never preferable. This is not to say that there is not a notion of indefiniteness (or incompleteness, as Ackrill would say) in Aristotle's conception of relational being. There is. The task, though, is to understand how it is that each kind of relational entity—relational words, metaphysical predicates, relative items, and so forth—expresses and exhibits both incompleteness and complementarity. It is this task that Morales's interpretation of indefiniteness fails adequately to support.

4.4 Disparity Between the Commentators' Interpretations

As we have seen, the commentators disagree about which entity it is that Aristotle regards as meeting the categorical requirements for relational being. For example, Ackrill and Morales think that relatives are actual concrete relational items. Ackrill 1963, 78 acknowledges that in Aristotle's efforts at classification Aristotle pays attention to how words are used, but Ackrill insists that the "categories classify things, not words" (73) and that Aristotle is not "engaged in a study of expressions" (79).

Morales agrees with Ackrill that Aristotle's overall emphasis in the *Categories* is on concrete items, not predicates, and that the focus of *Categories* 7, likewise, is on concrete relational items. On the other hand, Mignucci believes that "in *Categories* 7 [Aristotle] is interested in defining and discussing relatives in the sense of relational properties" (Mignucci 1986, 103). Mignucci considers the property being a slave to be the relative, and not, as Ackrill would have it, the slave Callias under a relational description.

One cause of the disparity between the commentators stems from Aristotle's lack of a precise terminology of relation. I noted earlier that Aristotle does not have separate words for 'relation' and 'relative'. He works around this partly by relying on the grammatical features of the Greek to do the work of conveying what he sees as a basic feature of relationality, i.e., a thing's being *of* or *than* or being somehow related to something.

Cavarnos 1975, however, relies too much on this grammatical feature in his commentary on *L* and *E* from *Categories* 7. He apparently sees the main distinction between *L* and *E* as a grammatical or linguistic one. He translates *E* as "relations are those entities whose very existence consists in their being in some way or other *towards* some other thing" (Cavarnos 1975, 44; italics Cavarnos). He then suggests that instead of just the two definitions of relational being Aristotle gives in *Categories* 7, each reflective of relations that are expressed, he says, in the genitive and accusative cases, Aristotle might have given a third definition based on cases where the relation is expressed in the dative case. Clearly much more is at stake with Aristotle's *E* formulation of relational being than the linguistic concerns Cavarnos wishes to mark.

Sometimes, though, commentators do have to confront the frequently unavoidable, but not insurmountable, ambiguity of the Greek itself. This can lead to some difficulty in translating, and thus, in interpreting the text. For example, nouns are often unaccompanied in the Greek by either definite or indefinite articles. Thus *anthrōpos* may be translated as the species or secondary substance "man" or as the primary substance "a man", i.e., "an individual man". As I mentioned in Chapter 2, the use of *tis* often serves to emphasize the particularity of an item as a primary, rather than a secondary, substance. So writing *"anthrōpos tis"*, then, as opposed to *"anthrōpos"* alone, allows one to indicate that an individual man is meant, or quite possibly that a certain kind of individual man is meant, say, a kind of man with a specific skill as opposed to just any man.

On the other hand, when the Greek definite article does appear it frequently is not translated into English. This leads to ambiguity which sometimes leads translators astray. At *Categories* 1b4, for instance, Aristotle gives examples of entities in the category of substance, i.e., a man and a horse (*"ho tis anthrōpos ē ho tis hippos"*). In my view Cooke 1938, 21 mistranslates this by translating each with inverted commas added, viz. 'man' and 'horse', thereby giving the impression that

Aristotle is concerned more about substance words than with the actual beings that are substances. And when Aristotle does include an article with relative words, we regularly are faced with having no failsafe way to detect when he is using as opposed to mentioning a word. In Aristotle's use of the Greek '*to diplasion*', for instance, it is sometimes difficult to discern whether he simply is mentioning the word 'double' or whether he means a concrete item that is double or the relational property or metaphysical predicate double.

The disparity among the commentators' views also stems from a more serious and stubborn problem, one exacerbated by the aforementioned ambiguities: disagreement as to what Aristotle's categorial project is in the *Categories*. Because concrete beings are the most real entities for Aristotle, it is easy to see them as looming over Aristotle's categorial project. Their importance to Aristotle leads commentators understandably to select them as obvious candidates for genuine categorical relatives.

As I suggested in Chapter 1, the *Categories* represents Aristotle's effort at juggling three chores at once: examining the beings that actually exist, the manners in which they exist, and the way in which these are knowable as conceptual units of thought in and through language. My view is that all three tasks take on different degrees of importance to Aristotle throughout the *Categories* and that his project encompasses all three. We must take care, then, to note the interplay of linguistic, metaphysical, ontological, and logical issues surrounding each category, but the category of relation requires our extra care. It requires extra care first, because the category encompasses the most peculiar of Aristotelian entities, the least real of all Aristotelian entities—entities most in need of help to become "real" or actual entities—and second, because of the unusual ontological requirements for the instantiation of relatives as concrete entities.

Commentaries on Aristotle's theory of relation nearly all suffer, I think, from a failure to account for the subtle shifts of focus of Aristotle's concerns and how these shifts should affect our analysis of Aristotle's relatives. As we saw with Morales's commentary, he makes a single interpretation of the indefiniteness of relational being range over Aristotle's diverse treatment of relational words, attributes, grammatical predicates, and actual relations. While I agree that Aristotle is trying to account for the natural relationality of all relational being, we cannot analyze the various relational entities evident in Aristotle's relational theory without carefully taking into account the peculiar relational behavior, as it were, of the kinds of relational entity

Aristotle's theory encompasses. Now to varying degrees all the commentators do acknowledge that Aristotle alludes to more than one kind of relational entity (relational words, metaphysical relational attributes, concrete relational items, and so forth). In my opinion, however, none of the commentators distinguishes as carefully as they ought to between when they think Aristotle is considering one kind of relational entity as opposed to another kind. And none of them discusses with much care the feature I believe crucial to unlocking Aristotle's relational theory, namely, Aristotle's *E* formulation of relational being.

In the next few Sections, I present what I think is a better approach to analyzing the relational character of the various relational entities implied in Aristotle's relational theory. I then will present my own analysis of Aristotle's relatives which builds upon the good aspects of the commentaries I have examined and attempts to ameliorate some of their deficiencies.

4.5 Aristotelian Entities and Their Relational Characteristics

We know Aristotle's basic intuition about the complementarity or relationality of all relational entities: We see it in the *L* and *E* criteria; we observe it in the schema for classes of relations in the *Metaphysics*: relational being always entails the relationship of one thing to another. The task now is to better understand the various ways in which Aristotle both conceives of and expects these ways of being relational to behave in actual relational contexts

Now, in some sense, all entities besides primary entities are relational in that they have with their subjects a relation of predication or inherence. We know, however, that relational non-substantial entities differ fundamentally from non-relational non-substantial entities. Relational entities have a more complicated relationship with their subjects. What I aim to show in this Section is just how relational entities differ, not only from non-relational non-substantial entities, but from other sorts of relational entities as well.

One good way to begin this task is to situate Aristotle's relatives against the backdrop of the other Aristotelian entities vis-à-vis their relational characteristics.[27] I differentiate the entities by the dependence they have or do not have on other entities. There are six kinds of entity to consider:

[1]   Primary substances, i.e., things that are not dependent upon other entities for their existence.

[2]   Secondary substances, i.e., things that are dependent upon some subject for their existence but do not inhere in any subject.

[3]   Non-relational non-substantial entities, i.e., accidents that inhere in other entities and are existentially dependent upon one other entity.

[4]   *L* entities (relational entities and pseudo-relational entities that meet the first four marks of relational being, [M1]-[M4]), i.e., accidents that inhere in other entities and depend on each other for their reciprocal, linguistic existence, but are not existentially dependent upon each other.

[5]   *E* entities, i.e., metaphysical relational entities that meet *L* and are unilaterally and reciprocally dependent upon each other for their metaphysical existence.

[6]   *E** entities (instantiated, actual relational entities that meet *E* as well as the six marks of relational being, [M1]-[M6]), i.e., things that are unilaterally dependent upon an underlying subject and are reciprocally dependent upon another entity and that entity's underlying subject in order to exist.[28]

Primary substances are the only entities that are not dependent upon other entities in Aristotle's the meta-ontological framework. Secondary substances are said of other entities and thus have a predicational dependence on those entities as subjects, but they do not inhere in those subjects. Non-substantial entities that are non-relational inhere in other entities and so depend on them for their existence.

We now come to the relational non-substantial entities. I will begin by discussing *L* entities. As *legomena*, i.e., conceptual thought-units, it is clear that all relatives can be expressed through speech as relational words and that they can be used to form grammatical relational predicates.

All relatives are incomplete in that they must have a reference to some entity to be completive. Since according to the *Categories* 7 account of relational being all relatives must have their reciprocating correlative, *L* relatives are linguistically dependent on each other. I use the word 'linguistic' here in a broad sense which encompasses the grammatical rules and conventions Aristotle notes in *Categories* 7 for recognizing relatives (e.g., that relatives are said to be *of* or *than* something). *L* entities, however, are only pseudo-relational accidents as they are relational words or names. Thus, a mention of an appropriate correlative word fulfills the needed relational complement for the *L* relative.

Moreover, *L* entities are linguistically dependent on each other but I also use the word to highlight the semantic or intensional features of relative as conceptual thought-units. Aristotle acknowledges that the meaning of a relative cannot be ascertained apart from the meaning its correlative expression, e.g., we cannot define 'double' without mentioning 'half' (see *Topics* 142a28–31 and *Sophistical Refutations* 181b25–28).

It is this linguistic dependence that *L* relatives have with each other that makes it seem as though the parts of secondary substance are genuine relatives. We may speak of the "cow of Mrs. O'Leary", but 'cow' is not a relative even though it meets *L*'s linguistic criteria for relational being.

Next, there are *E* entities. An *E* relative is a non-substantial, non-instantiated entity. I am interpreting *E* relatives as metaphysical relational predicates. We learned from *Categories* 7 that being an *E* entity involves "holding in some way towards" something. That is, every *E* entity constitutes a "holding somehow" of something, say, *x*, to something else, *y*. The key feature of an *E* entity is this holding somehow component which acts, I believe, as a quasi-logical relational predicate, which I will describe further below in Section 4.7.

At *Categories* 8a38 ff. a crucial turning point occurs where Aristotle moves to an examination of cases or instances of relatives. He uses the expression *tode ti* which translates in a variety of ways including "a certain this" or "a this particular thing" which suggests he is taking into consideration the way in which relational entities behave, as it were, in actual relational contexts. Actual realities are concrete or instantiated realities for Aristotle. Actual relational entities, then, are concrete or instantiated *E* relatives entities. I am calling these instantiated *E* entities *E** relatives. But as instantiated *E* relatives, *E** relatives do not simply exist as concrete items that possess a relational predicate. For *E** entities to exist, certain conditions must be met. I concur with Mignucci (1986) and Morales (1994) in what this entails. *E** relatives are unilaterally dependent upon an underlying subject and are reciprocally dependent upon another entity and that entity's underlying subject. So, for an *E** entity to exist it must be related to the ground of the relative and the ground of the correlative. There also must be the relational property that effects the "holding somehow" together of the two items relationally.

In my view, each relational entity (L relatives, E relatives, and E^* relatives) should to be analyzed with an eye toward the unique ways in which each kind of entity is relational. A distinction, then, needs to be drawn between abstract metaphysical relatives, i.e., E relatives, and actual relative entities, i.e., E^* relatives. Each exhibits its incompleteness differently and should be analyzed with this in mind. Morales (1994) indicates the importance of the indefiniteness (as he puts it) of relational being. In Section 4.3, I discussed the difficulties with Morales's interpretation of this feature. I do agree with Morales that the incompleteness or "gappiness" of relational being something critical to Aristotle's conception of relational being. The central error Morales makes is in not distinguishing carefully between the kinds of incompleteness Aristotle's account of relatives involves, i.e., between the different incompleteness of L, E, and E^* relational being. Distinguishing as I have done between E and E^* relatives allows us to better note the metaphysical requirements of relational being and will help us to work out in a more pragmatic way, what it means for E^* relatives to have the ontological dependence they have on their subjects.

4.6 Recurrent and Non-Recurrent Non-Substantial Entities

This issue of the ontological and metaphysical dependence of non-substantial entities on their subjects leads to the question of whether non-substantial entities in general and relatives in particular are recurrent or non-recurrent entities. The debate about the issue is epic in length and falls beyond the scope of my investigations here. Interestingly, it has negligible bearing on my analysis of Aristotle's relational theory.

In brief, the debate is as follows: Both sides accept Aristotle's view that without primary substances, i.e., concrete items, none of the other entities (secondary substances and any of the non-substantial entities) could exist (see *Categories* 2a35–2b1). There is a problem, however, about whether the non-substantial items that inhere in some subjects but are not said of any subjects are recurrent or non-recurrent particulars. Aristotle says that a Type-2 item, i.e., a item that is in a subject but not in it as a part of a subject, cannot exist separately from its subject and is not said of a subject (see *Categories* 1a23–25). A Type-2 item would be, for instance, the individual bit of white inhering in a subject. Some scholars, e.g., Ackrill (1963), Allen (1969), and Wedin (1993), generally believe that Type-2 items are non-recurrent non-substantial particulars. They believe that since a Type-2 item cannot exist separately from its subject, it cannot occur in many subjects. Type-2 entities only exist instantiated in their individual subjects.

Here is an example to illustrate the non-recurrent position. Suppose we take what appear to be three identically colored white golf balls. What we actually have, they would say, are three golf balls each with a distinct and unique shade of white: golf ball white^1, golf ball white^2, and golf ball white^3. Each shade of white is a non-recurrent entity for the shade of white inhering in each golf ball is not just one more instance of that shade of white recurring over and over again in multiple golf balls. Rather, once one of these balls is destroyed, its shade of white, say, the metaphysical predicate golf ball white^2, is also destroyed.

Other scholars, e.g., Furth 1988 and Owen 1965, consider Type-2 entities as recurrent non-substantial particulars. They would say that the color golf ball white is a universal, and that the white in each golf ball is a particular, recurrent instance, i.e., a token, of the universal golf ball white. The instances of golf ball white inhering in the three golf balls are thus the same white. So as long as some item has golf ball white inhering in it, the universal golf ball white, exists.

How does this debate affect our interpretation of Aristotle's relatives? Let us take the relative slave. The recurrent position would be that the property, being a slave, inheres in Rachel just as it inheres in Peggy. And when Rachel is no longer a slave, the metaphysical predicate continues to subsist so long as some slave actually exists. On the non-recurrent view, Rachel's being a slave means that the property, say, being a slave^1 or perhaps slaveness in Rachel, inheres in her, whereas the property of being a slave that Peggy has would be being a slave^2 or slaveness is Peggy.

As to which side I will cast my lot, I remain undecided. Both positions are compatible with the above framework I have offered of Aristotle's relatives. Both *E* relatives and *E** relatives may be conceived of as recurrent or non-recurrent entities. As a recurrent entity, an *E* relative corresponds to a universal relational entity with the *E** relative being its token or instance inhering in a particular item. On the non-recurrent reading, the *E* relative corresponds to the metaphysical predicate whose sole instantiation would correspond to the *E** relative. Neither account favors or disfavors my interpretation of relatives.

4.7 Relatives as Complex Predicative Entities

I have suggested that our analysis of Aristotle's relatives should pay close attention to two interpretative stages: that of interpreting *E* relatives and *E** relatives. Interpreting *E* relatives requires taking due consideration of the holding somehow component and its function as a something akin to a logical relational predicate. If I am correct in interpreting the holding somehow component of *E* as functioning as a quasi-logical relational predicate of sorts, then what Aristotle is saying here is that whenever a relational predicate or universal is instantiated, some minimally dyadic relation is instantiated as well. That is, there is a relation (i.e., a "holding somehow") between or involving one item and another item.

In Chapter 2, I described the holding somehow component of *E*. I mentioned that the construction isolates something that in modern logic would be akin to a logical relational predicate or relational function in the sentence '*x* is R of *y*' where 'R' stands for any *E*-compliant relational attribute. Let me elaborate on it further.

I illustrate the logical incompleteness of the pre-instantiated *E* relative below in (26) 'R' indicates the *E* entity's "holding somehow," and the variables '*x*' and '*y*' indicate the things to which the *E* relative is in some way related:

(26)   *x*   is R of   *y*

The variables '*x*' and '*y*' represent the logical gaps that must be filled for the relative to be realized. In this regard, 'R' stands as a relational indicator, indicating that instantiation will be incomplete without solving for '*x*' and '*y*'.

As I mentioned above, as instantiated items, *E** relatives do not exist solely as concrete items that simply possess a relational predicate of some kind. To think that they only exist in this way is to restrict ourselves to a monadic analysis of them, an analysis which is only concerned to account for a subject and its accident. A more comprehensive analysis must accommodate Aristotle's own conditions for the existence of *E** entities. *E** relatives logically and ontologically are unilaterally dependent upon an underlying subject, and logically are dependent upon still another entity and its underlying subject. When we analyze them in this way, we see that a certain degree of logical complexity is involved because an *E** entity logically identifies the constituents of a concrete relation. The relational proposition "Peggy is a slave of Tucker" in (27) illustrates this. Here, '*ri*' indicates a relative item, '*ci*' the correlative item and '*CRP*' the complex relative predicate:

(27)   Peggy   is a slave of   Tucker
        ri   *CRP*   *ci*

Peggy's fundamental existence is as a primary substance, not as a relative. She is, though, the underlying subject or ground for the relative and as such E^* counts her as the relative item (*ri*). But because every relative must have its correlative item (*ci*), the complex relational predicate must also be allied to that thing of which the relative is spoken. I call the relative predicate "complex" because of the logical burden the predicate must bear of being relationally dependent on both grounds of the relative items.

An analysis of E^* relatives demands the analysis of the three logical elements: two subjects and the relational property that brings them together relationally. The difficulty, of course, is to interpret the relative's ontological character as an accident of some single subject, while providing an analysis that meets the demands of accounting for both logical terms as the grounds of the referent and correlative items.

Critics believe that since relatives are simple predicates or accidents, the propositions "Peggy is a singer" and "Peggy is a slave" will have the same subject-predicate logical form, F(*x*), and share the same substance-accident metaphysic. But it should be clearer now why a simple monadic analysis of the proposition does such a poor job of capturing Aristotle's view of relation. From a logical point of view, the monadic predicate F(*x*) adequately evinces the general logical dimensions of Aristotle's substance-accident ontology, but it fails to account for the dyad of relative and correlative items that Aristotle so adamantly insists every relational predicate encompass. Given Aristotle's concern for properly accounting for the dyadic behavior of relatives, and his ontological requirements for actual relational existents, the correct analysis of "Peggy is a slave of Tucker" can hardly be limited to symbolizing the predication of the property <u>slave</u> of Peggy and symbolizing it as '$S(x)$'.

My basic disagreement with viewing Aristotle's relatives from a monadic perspective, is that it does a poor job accounting for what Aristotle tells us about relational being. The analysis of relational being Aristotle describes in *Categories* 7 is best explained by the dyadic relationality of the relative-correlative pairs. But more important, it allows us to make better sense of Aristotle's conception of relational being. And though monadism remains indispensable for analyzing the other non-substantial accidents, it also obscures the way Aristotle conceives of the dyadic quality of relational being.

4.8 Summary

In Chapter 4 I have examined interpretations of Aristotle's accounts of relatives Ackrill (1963), Mignucci (1986), and Morales (1994) and pointed out difficulties with each one. In my own analysis of Aristotle's relatives, I showed how E represents Aristotle's view of the dyadic nature of relational being. Taken as a complex relational predicate, an E relative behaves as a dyadic relational predicate. I have suggested that we distinguish two stages of analysis to assist us in getting a better understanding of Aristotle's relational theory.

My analysis takes due consideration of categorical relatives as the two kinds of relational entity: first, metaphysically, as non-substantial E entities, and second, onto-logically, as accidents of substance viewed as complex relational predicates. I have also offered some views as to how Aristotle expects these entities to behave, as it were, both as metaphysical relational predicates, i.e., universals, and as instantiated relational predicates. My analysis reconciles Aristotle's consideration of relational being (a) as concrete E^* relative items, (b) as predicative relational accidents of substance, and (c) as non-substantial E entities. Proceeding in this way provides a better way of understanding the key predicative and logical characteristics of relatives. Once again, I believe that our findings continue to show that Aristotle unquestionably had some insight into the dyadic nature of relational being.

Next, I turn to the epistemological considerations of Aristotle's relational theory.

Chapter 5

Epistemological Considerations of Aristotle's Relatives

In Chapter 5, I take up the epistemological issues that stem mainly from Aristotle's *Categories* account of relational being. My strategy for Chapter 5 is as follows. First, I review Aristotle's substance argument, his argument for excluding substance from the category of relation.

After reviewing the substance argument, I present an overview of the knowing definitely criterion, which Aristotle says follows from *E*, i.e., the revised account of relational being. In Aristotle's view, since being for a relative means for it to hold in some way toward another thing, it will also be the case that if one knows definitely that a thing is a relative, one will also know definitely that thing to which the relative stands in relation. Thus, he thinks that if a particular thing definitely is known to be a relative, then its correlative must also be known definitely. I follow this overview of the knowing definitely criterion by examining commentary on it by Ackrill (1963), Mignucci (1986), and Morales (1994). I then discuss why the knowing definitely criterion helps Aristotle's substance argument to succeed.

Finally, at the end of Chapter 5, I briefly take up the problem of reconciling two seemingly contradictory positions Aristotle has with respect to the knowing definitely criterion: He insists in *Categories* 7 that relatives be known definitely and yet he maintains in *Metaphysics*

V.15 that indefinite numerical relational entities be included in the category of relation. I do not resolve the matter, but rather give a number of considerations that I believe count in favor of reconciling the two positions.

5. Aristotle's Substance Argument

The first account of relational being, L, allowed the parts of primary substance to count as relatives. Aristotle introduces E because he thinks it will bar the parts of primary substances, or any substance for that matter, from the category. He also thinks the knowing definitely criterion follows as a consequence of E. Since only genuine relatives meet the knowing definitely criterion and the parts of substance fail to meet it, Aristotle contends that the parts of substance are not relatives. Here again is a sketch of the substance argument (SA) Aristotle offers at *Categories* 7.

SA1   For something to be a relative, it must be related to something, i.e., it must hold in some way toward something (8a31-33).

SA2   If one knows definitely that a particular thing is a relative, then one also will know definitely that thing to which it is holding somehow (8a37-8b4).

SA3   If one does not know that to which something is related, neither will one know whether it is related to something (8b9).

SA4   One can know definitely that something is a head without having to know that to which it is related (8b15-19).

SA5   Therefore, heads (and other primary substances) are not relatives (8b19-21).

SA6   Since no primary substance is a relative, no secondary substance is a relative either (8a15; see also 2a34–2b5).

SA7   Therefore, no substance is a relative (8b20–21).

The substance argument presents several epistemological difficulties. For instance, how do genuine relatives satisfy the knowing definitely criterion? Or put the other way around: how does the criterion help isolate genuine relatives from the pseudo-relatives? What does "knowing definitely" a relative involve? Why does Aristotle think that we can know that something is a head without knowing whose head it is, while we cannot know, e.g., that someone is a slave without knowing who her master is?

The first step in answering the above questions will be to begin by presenting an overview of the knowing definitely criterion described at *Categories* 8a35–8b14. Next, I discuss why Aristotle believes the knowing definitely criterion is a consequence of *E*. Following that, I consider what it is that we are supposed to know definitely, i.e., the epistemic target of the criterion, and what the character or epistemic force of the definiteness is. Then I explain why the knowing definitely criterion does not apply to the parts of primary substance. Throughout I present commentary on the *aporia* and the knowing definitely criterion by Ackrill (1963), Mignucci (1986), and Morales (1994). Although no one of commentators arrives at a fully satisfactory account, I show that together they move us closer to a plausible analysis of Aristotle's argument.

5.1 Overview of the Knowing Definitely Criterion

Recall that after raising the *aporia* about the parts of some substances being able to be included in the category of relation, Aristotle presents *E*, his revised account of relational being.

> But if it [i.e., the former formulation] was inadequate and if those things are relative for which being is the same as holding in some way toward something (*esti ta pros ti hois to einai tauton esti tō pros ti pōs echein*), then perhaps some answer may be found [i.e., some way of excluding substance from the category]. The previous definition holds good for all relatives, but indeed this—their being called *of* other things—is not the same as what their being relatives is. (*Categories* 8a31–35)

The being component and the holding somehow component of *E* allows Aristotle to offer the categorical formula for relational being: To be a relative entity that entity must meet the special meta-ontological requirements of dependence upon the relative's correlative and the subject of both the relative and its correlative. Aristotle says it is clear from *E* that

> From the above [i.e., the second formulation of relational being] it is clear that if someone knows definitely that a thing is one of the relatives he will also know definitely that in relation to which it is spoken of. This is evident even on the face of it. For if someone knows of a certain thing (*tis tode ti*) that it is one of the relatives, and being for [relatives] is the same thing as holding somehow in relation to a thing, he also knows that toward which it is holding somehow. (*Categories* 8a36-8b3)

The epistemological criterion that emerges from *E*, I have called the "knowing definitely criterion":

The knowing definitely criterion

> If a certain thing definitely is known to be a relative, then its correlative must also be known definitely. (*Categories* 8a36–8b3

There are two things we must assess: the epistemic target and force of the criterion. The first step to take in determining what it means to have definite knowledge of a relative is to settle on which relational entity is the appropriate epistemic target for the knowing definitely criterion. As my investigation in Chapter 4 revealed, there is more than one kind of relational entity to consider. The second step is to ascertain the epistemic force of the criterion.

The Epistemic Target of the Knowing Definitely Criterion

To identify the epistemic target of the criterion depends on how we interpret Aristotle's relational entities. In Chapter 4, I argued for making a distinction between Aristotle's consideration of metaphysical relational being and his more pragmatic consideration of how relatives behave in actual relational contexts. By adopting this distinction, I identified two kinds of categorical relatives: *E* and *E** relatives. But which one of these relatives is the epistemic target of the knowing definitely criterion?

Aristotle gives double and more beautiful as examples of the kinds of relatives that meet the knowing definitely criterion (*Categories* 8b8-9). If the epistemic target of the criterion is a an *E* relative, i.e., a metaphysical predicate or relational attribute, such as being double, the criterion will involve knowing definitely that being double entails being double of some half. Similarly, in the case of being more beautiful, if the epistemic target is knowing definitely a metaphysical predicate, the criterion will involve knowing definitely that whatever is more beautiful, is more beautiful than something than its correlative predicate, what is less beautiful. I will call this the metaphysical interpretation of the criterion. As Aristotle says (*Topics* 142a26-32), one can hardly define, or give an account of a genuine relative, without including its correlative in that account. So under the metaphysical interpretation, what one needs to have is conceptual knowledge of relational attributes and their correlatives.

If our epistemic target is an E^*relative, i.e., a concrete relative item, the knowing definitely criterion will entail knowing the exact correlative object or concrete item that stands in relation to the relative. I will call this the objectual interpretation of the criterion. Under the objectual interpretation knowing definitely that Peggy is a slave entails knowing definitely that Peggy is a slave of Tucker.

The Epistemic Force of the Knowing Definitely Criterion

With respect to the epistemic force of the knowing definitely criterion, Aristotle mentions five degrees of epistemic certainty at *Categories* 8a37–8b21. They are: (a) supposition (*huplēpsis*), (b) knowledge (*epistēmē*), (c) knowing definitely (*hōrismenōs eidenai*), (d) knowing indefinitely (*aphōrismenōs oiden, aoristōs eisetai*), and (e) certain knowledge (*eidenai akribōs*). Aristotle does not explicitly state which option he has in mind. However, we can eliminate immediately two of the options. First, we can eliminate (d) knowing indefinitely as a candidate because the whole point of the criterion is to knowing definitely. We also can eliminate (a) supposition. The sense of supposition here at *Categories* 8b10 is that of an unwarranted or careless guess. It is not the honest mistake a witness makes when saying that one tattoo on the suspect's right arm was that of a tiger instead of a leopard. This is an example of someone believing, but not knowing, something is the case. So, neither (a) nor (d) is an instance of definite knowledge.

Which of the remaining options best captures the epistemic force of the knowing definitely criterion: (b) knowledge, (c) knowing definitely, or (e) certain knowledge? Aristotle does not indicate which it is, but here, at least, he evidently holds all three on a par. First, there is no reason to believe that Aristotle is using (b) *epistēmē* in its technical sense of scientific knowledge. Rather, he seems instead to have in mind the notion of genuine or actual knowledge as opposed to supposition. The same distinction most likely is at work with (c) knowing definitely and (e) certain knowledge. Aristotle may be appealing to the notion of someone having specific knowledge of something, such as one would have when one knows the definition of something or has a complete account of it. For instance, if I do not know the differentia in my definition of *F*, then I cannot know definitely the definition (or essence) of *F*. Even if knowledge of a definition is not what Aristotle is after, he clearly is again trying to distinguish supposition from a much more certain and sure knowledge. This latter is in keeping with the example he gives at *Categories* 8b12-13: It does no good merely to suppose that there exists something more beautiful than a particular thing without knowing what it is that thing is being compared to. It may very well be the case that there does not exist anything less beautiful than that thing.

Whichever interpretation we take, the objectual or the metaphysical, impacts significantly on how we should understand the knowing definitely criterion, its target and its force. It is one thing to grasp definitely the concept of something being more beautiful and understand that when something is more beautiful there is also something that exists which is less beautiful, it is another thing to be forced to identify precisely which slave belongs to a certain master. With the above overview of the knowing definitely criterion in hand, I turn now to each commentator's interpretation of the knowing definitely criterion and his evaluation of the substance argument.

5.2 Ackrill's Interpretation of the Knowing Definitely Criterion

Ackrill has serious reservations about the knowing definitely criterion. Ackrill states that *L* allows one to know that something is a relative without specifically knowing its correlative. The knowing definitely criterion, on the other hand, raises the bar unnecessarily high, in his view, by excluding some relational terms that clearly belong in the category of relation. Ackrill adopts the objectual interpretation of the knowing definitely criterion. Consequently, he thinks meeting the criterion requires specifying the exact item that is the correlative item to the relative. So, knowing definitely that *x* is a slave requires knowing definitely who is *x*'s master.

> However, this would make the criterion too strong, since it would not be satisfied by indisputably relative terms like 'half' and 'slave': one

can know that 97 is half some other number without knowing what that number is, and that Callias is a slave without knowing who his master is. (Ackrill 1963, 102)

One immediately feels sympathetic to Ackrill's lament that the knowing definitely criterion is too strong. Why should it be impossible to know that 97 is half of some number without know what it is half of? Certainly we can appeal to the laws of mathematics for they allow us to assert that a given number is half of some other number. For Ackrill, we do not need exact knowledge of 194 to know that it is double of 97 or that 97 is the half of 194.

As I will discuss further below, Morales thinks that with E and the knowing definitely criterion Aristotle is establishing the necessary and sufficient conditions by which relatives may exist. Morales suggests that Ackrill's analysis begins from a difference perspective. Morales believes Ackrill starts from the perspective of already having been confronted with the items under consideration: for example, the slave, Callias. I am inclined to agree with Morales's suspicions about Ackrill's approach. Morales assesses Ackrill's counter-examples this way:

> . . . But in each of these counter-examples we are assuming that a relative exists (e.g. because someone has told us, or because we are acquainted with a general mathematical law); we are not inferring its existence from the basic elements that *constitute* the relation. Aristotle, on the contrary is trying to specify the necessary and sufficient conditions for a relative to *exist* (to be) (Morales 1994, 263; italics Morales)

Perhaps someone has told us that Callias is a slave and we believe that report. On the basis of this report, we may be prepared to affirm that Callias is indeed a slave without our having to know *exactly* who is his master. This is not how Aristotle sees things, though. For even if we agree that knowledge claims about numbers can be made based not on definite knowledge of the numbers involved, but rather on the general laws of mathematics, the case with masters and slaves is different. Here general knowledge of what masters are allows one to know that masters are masters *of* slaves, but it does not allow us to claim that a certain (*tis tode ti*) individual is a slave.

Ackrill attempts to ameliorate the knowing definitely criterion and its impact on the substance argument. I discuss his attempts in the next Section.

Ackrill's Interpretation of the Substance Argument

In Ackrill's commentary, he proposes three ways of handling the criterion's epistemic demands such that it offers a reasonable explanation of how heads fail to meet the criterion. In the end, Ackrill will reject all the possibilities he proposes and find that the substance argument does not succeed.

Ackrill believes that the knowing definitely criterion is too strong. Yet he begins by suggesting that we simply knuckle down and hold ourselves accountable to the strict requirement of definitely knowing the correlative item. The problem here, as Ackrill sees it (Ackrill 1963, 102), is that there is no good reason why this criterion is waived in the case of 'head' or 'hand'. If definitely knowing that Peggy is a slave entails knowing that Tucker is her master, why does not definitely knowing that this is a head entail knowing whose head it is? Ackrill sees no reason why the two cases occasion such different epistemic demands.

Next, Ackrill suggests that we try to sidestep the issue and consider something a relative as long as someone (maybe not me) knows, or could know, who or what the correlate is.

> We might try watering down the strong criterion so as to allow that one may know that *A* is *R* without knowing what it is *R* of, it being required only that *someone* knows what it is *R* of or that one (or someone) *could* find out what it is *R* of. (Ackrill 1963, 102; italics Ackrill)

Setting aside for a moment that Aristotle thinks unattached heads are heads in name only, Ackrill hypothesizes that since a head must be someone's head someone will know whose head it was. In other words, I may not know whose head it was in the basket beneath the guillotine, but Madame Lafarge (or someone else) does. This sort of "surrogate" knowing might take the edge off the criterion by no longer requiring that everyone in every instance be able to know definitely both relata of the relation. However, Ackrill remarks that this approach would have the deleterious effect of again allowing heads and hands to meet the criterion. If they can still be known by someone, then they pass the criterion by virtue of some surrogate knower's knowledge of what they are. Because they can be known in this manner the interpretation must be rejected as unacceptable.

I agree that Aristotle probably does not have this sort of surrogate knowing in mind, but not for the reasons Ackrill mentions. The fact that someone other than myself might know definitely whose head it is in the guillotine has no bearing on whether such substances meet the knowing definitely criterion and count as E^* relatives.

Now Ackrill is right if he is following the received text at *Categories* 8b18-19 which says that "it is not possible" to know definitely whose head it is. He is not right, however, if we accept his own emendation (see Ackrill 1963, 23). The emended text says that "it is not necessary" to know definitely whose head it is to know that it is a head. Aristotle's point is not that someone could not know definitely whose head it is; his point is that a head can be known for the very thing that it is *without* someone having to know whose head it is. The point is that it is not necessary for someone—no matter who that knower is—to know whose head it is in order to know that a head is a human head. What is at stake is knowing that it is a human head, for instance, as opposed to a horse head or a basketball or any other item.

Last, Ackrill wonders whether Aristotle is distinguishing between (a) those items that must actually exist together to be related, as with slave and master, and (b) those that need only potentially exist together in order to be relational. Ackrill suggests that even though 'boat' occurs in the definition of 'rudder', neither item actually has to exist with the other for the item either to be what it is or to be known for what it is. This would mean that being a slave actually requires Peggy to have a master, whereas being a rudder would not require the rudder actually to be part of a boat to be a rudder (Ackrill 1963, 102).

Ackrill admits that this is unlikely to be Aristotle's position. Ackrill rejects the actuality-potentiality distinction by raising two issues: (1) the incompleteness of relative expressions and (2) the functional integrity of substance. First, Ackrill notes that L-relative expressions are incomplete expressions such as "larger _____" and "similar _____." (Ackrill 1963, 98–99, 102). Second, he remarks that "there is no hint that the criterion would be satisfied by terms which have only the sort of definitional dependence which 'rudder' has on 'boat'" (102–103).

If I understand his point, Ackrill thinks that since E relatives must also meet L, relatives that are definitionally dependent on each other are not incomplete enough to meet L. And since they cannot be L relatives, they cannot be E relatives either.

Ackrill makes it sound as though it were a drawback for definitionally related expressions (boat-rudder, head-body) to fail the incompleteness requirements of L and E. But there is a good reason why they fail. Aristotle never proposes that 'rudder' and 'boat' are genuine relative expressions because neither exhibits the necessary

reciprocity he demands of relational expressions (See *Categories* 6b39–
7a23; 7b2–14). 'Boat' is not an incomplete expression. Whatever
definitional dependence 'rudder' may have on 'boat' Aristotle eschews
for the contrived relational schema of 'rudder' and 'ruddered'. Hence, a
'rudder' is "a rudder of a ruddered." At *Categories* 7a1–4 Aristotle also
employs this maneuver with bird and wing, saying that "a wing is a
wing of a winged."

Furthermore, it is just such cases of part-whole relationships (e.g.,
rudder-boat, head-body, and all the others that obtain between the parts
of secondary substance and secondary substance) that Aristotle means
to exclude from the category of genuine relatives. It is not surprising,
then, that "there is no hint" of them satisfying either of Aristotle's
relational criteria.

Ackrill is right, however, that definitionally dependent items are
too complete to be E relational. As we will see below, Mignucci and
Morales exploit this semantic feature in their commentaries to explain
how a head can be known as Aristotle suggests. Ackrill does not seize
the chance.

Second, Ackrill reminds us that for Aristotle a severed finger or a
dislodged eye is a finger or an eye in name only (Metaphysics
1035b23–25). Ackrill argues persuasively that Aristotle cannot mean
that a head can exist as a head while needing only potentially to be
attached to a body. This is indeed correct. Nevertheless, what may be at
issue here is not the separability of a head or a hand, but rather, its
ability to be recognized and known for "the very thing that it is"
without our having to know either its specific or would-be correlate. If
this is correct, then our worry about the inconsistency of Aristotle's
views on the matter is moot.

Overall Ackrill's analysis is hampered by his objectual
interpretation of the knowing definitely criterion, and in the end he
finds no suitable way to lessen its demands and, thus, sees no
satisfactory support for Aristotle's substance argument.

5.3 Mignucci's Interpretation of the Knowing Definitely Criterion

Mignucci (1986) believes that the objectual, or what he calls the
"traditional" interpretation of the knowing definitely criterion is wrong.

> It is so obviously false that it is difficult to believe that Aristotle could
> have been committed to it. Take a number, say 1,515,798. I can
> immediately state that it is the double of some number, even if I do not

know exactly what this number is. In order to say that it is the double of 757,899 I need to calculate it. Nevertheless, before carrying out the calculation, I can assert that the number at issue is the double of some number. Analogous counter-examples to this interpretation can be found by considering other instances of [*E* relatives], such as "son" or "slave". There are surely cases in which one can know that *a* is a slave without knowing exactly whose slave he is. (Mignucci 1986, 109)

While Mignucci agrees with Ackrill that one can know that a certain number is double, for instance, without having to know exactly what it is double of, he does not think that the knowing definitely criterion should be interpreted objectually. For Mignucci, Aristotle's examples at *Categories* 8a37–b5 are examples of relatives that are relational properties, not concrete items. While Mignucci 1986, 112 acknowledges that particular cases are being explored by Aristotle as is evident by Aristotle's use of the Greek expression "a certain this" ("*tode ti*"), he thinks knowing that a certain individual is one of the relatives means knowing that a certain *relational property* is one of the relatives.

But what does this entail precisely? Recall Mignucci's formal expression for *E* relatives includes a constitutive relation that is based on the meaning of the relative property in question. Mignucci notes, however, that knowing a relational property definitely does not entail knowing the definition of a relational property. Since heads and hands can be defined, they would pass the epistemic criterion and qualify as relatives.

> One should therefore be able to state a definition of "being a head" without mentioning, or even knowing, that it is intrinsically linked to something by a constitutive relation. But a definition of "being a head" in which no reference is made to its being a part of a living body can hardly be thought to be adequate by Aristotle's standards. (Mignucci 1986, 111)

Indeed, as Mignucci reminds us, for Aristotle

> a head severed from its body is no longer a head and therefore no longer satisfies the definition of being a head, since two homonymous properties do not have the same λόγος τῆς οὐσίας. (Mignucci 1986, 111)

Moreover, Mignucci rejects the notion that knowing a relational property means knowing that the property itself has a particular property (Mignucci 1986, 110). What Mignucci means is this. Take, for example, the relational property being double. Let us say that the property of being double has the property of being "twice as much as something." Now if I know that something has the property of being double, the knowing definitely criterion would require that I know it also has the property of being twice as much as something. The problem with this solution is that heads and hands could again pass this epistemic test because the property one gives for being a hand, for example, could be that of having the property of being attached to an arm. It is hard to see how one could know that something is a hand without knowing that this property—i.e., being attached to an arm—is something that hands satisfy.

What Mignucci does suggest is that the minimal requirement for meeting the criterion is that one must know the correlative item by means of the relational property's constitutive relation. What does this amount to? Minimally, one must know: (i) what the relational property entails, i.e., know that it has a constitutive relation, (ii) that an appropriate correlative object must exist, and (iii) that the correlative object entailed in the property's constitutive relation exists.

Mignucci does not think that the knowing definitely criterion is meant to be interpreted objectually. His analysis partially diffuses some of the epistemic pressure of the knowing definitely criterion by placing its general locus on properties, not particulars items. I say "partially" because on Mignucci's view the target of the criterion is not restricted to knowing just properties. On Mignucci's interpretation one still must know that the correlative object exists. *E* properties on his view are thus concretized and the items that serve to instantiate the relational property are subject to "certain knowledge" as well. In the end, then, knowing a property (and its relational entailments) requires of us as much as knowing specific correlatives does on the objectual interpretation. Although he earlier downplays Aristotle's concern with the items which are the grounds of relational properties, we see they are nevertheless vital to Mignucci's account of the knowing definitely criterion.

The epistemological force of the criterion, Mignucci says, concerns the quality of knowing, not the definiteness with which we must identify a specific object. Mignucci correctly states that "knowing definitely is a kind of [*epistēmē*], whose result is [*eidenai akribōs*]" or strict knowledge (see *Categories* 8b11–12; Mignucci 1986, 119). Since Aristotle holds supposition and indefinite knowledge on a par, Mignucci takes it that the distinction Aristotle is making is between belief and "real knowing" (Mignucci 1986, 120). What Aristotle rejects at *Categories* 8a8–12, Mignucci says, is the idea that one can know that a particular thing, x, has a relational property and at the same time only believe (and not know) that a relational property is truly predicated of x (Mignucci 1986, 118).

Mignucci's Interpretation of the Substance Argument

Mignucci appeals to the notion of stereotypes to account for the different epistemic standards Aristotle has for knowing that something is more beautiful and for knowing that something is a head (Mignucci 1986, 122–123). Mignucci suggests that all the knowing definitely criterion may require is that we have a stereotype of the word. He takes the relevant feature of stereotypes to be

> that they do not determine the extensions of the terms to which they are referred, but only permit us, at least in most cases, to say that a term is used with the same meaning even in different contexts. (Mignucci 1986, 122)

Even though a stereotype on Mignucci's view determines the meaning of a word, knowledge of meanings are not reducible to the knowledge of definitions, Mignucci says. I can know that Flipper is a dolphin without knowing the zoological definition of a dolphin. Similarly, knowing that something is a head does not require knowing the definition of a head. All that is involved in my knowing that "being a head" is true of an item, Mignucci states, is knowing the meaning of head, i.e., the stereotype that determines the meaning of head.

Mignucci offers a thought-experiment that purports to show how one can know what some secondary substances are without having to meet the demands of the knowing definitely criterion. Suppose that someone (Aldous) has a limited view of the goings on in the world. Aldous names an object a paw and makes certain propositions about the paw.

> [Aldous] succeeds in making the hold through which he is looking at the paws bigger, and he finally sees the whole dogs. He realizes that the objects that he probably considered before as independent items are parts of other objects and that his list of propositions about paws must be largely revised. But suppose that his list contained a proposition such a "s is a paw". Must this proposition be changed or rejected? I do not think so. This proves that one can know that s is a paw without knowing that a paw is a part of a living body. (Mignucci 1986, 125)

So, when Aldous is confronted with new information about the paws he has been viewing, e.g., that they are parts of a dog, this new information may force Aldous to revise the meaning he attributes to paws. Alternatively, Aldous may find that certain of his former propositions and, thus his stereotypes, remain true of paws.

Mignucci offers an objection to the above argument about paws. He begins by repeating the same experiment, this time with 'slave'. Aldous's stereotype for 'slave' omits the fact that slaves are possessions of masters.

> Suppose that Aldous can see only human beings who are slaves and that he decides to call them "slaves" without knowing the relation they have to other people. If in his list at this stage the proposition "k is a slave" appears, it will not be changed when Aldous knows that k is a slave of someone. Therefore, if in the case of paws we are able to conclude that one can know that s is a paw without knowing its constitutive relation, the same is true also for the case of slaves. (Mignucci 1986, 125)

The idea here is that Aldous' understanding of what a paw is gets better once he has a new bit of information about paws, but Mignucci believes that this new information is not essential for determining the meaning of 'paw'.

> The point I am trying to make is that our understanding of what being a paw is can be increased and improved by discovering that being a paw is always being a paw of something. The new piece of information joins what it is already known and is linked to it necessarily, but it is not essential for fixing the meaning of "paw" . . . [because] even before knowing that being a paw is a relative, we are able to have a stereotype of this entity that identifies it sufficiently. (Mignucci 1986, 125)

But Mignucci does not think we really can say the same for being a slave.

> Can we say the same for being a slave? I do not think so, because I cannot see what might constitute the core that identifies the meaning of "slave", if the information about its being in relation to something is lacking. . . . What really secures the meaning of "slave" is being in a certain relation to something. But, by hypothesis, this is not known to Aldous. Therefore the meanings of "slave" . . . before and after revision are different. . . . The discovery that people that he calls "slaves" have a constitutive relation to other people forces him to make

a revision of the meaning of the word "slave", if he wants to use it in the sense in which it is used in English. (Mignucci 1986, 126)

In the end, then, Aldous must change his stereotype of slave and include in it mention of this "new" fact.

I fail to see, though, how this experiment in truly bolsters Aristotle's substance argument. Mignucci does an admirable job of devising a way to account for the conceptual and objectual demands of the criterion by knowing the relational property and its constitutive relation. But does Mignucci's account of the knowing definitely criterion answer Ackrill's charge that the criterion is too strong? Mignucci's treatment offers a certain cachet of reasonableness to the epistemic demands that Aristotle makes. Clearly, there is nothing unreasonable in considering certain knowledge superior to mere belief. Moreover, the epistemic pressure of the criterion is no doubt partially relieved by placing its principal locus on properties, not particulars items. A head can be known for what it is on the basis of our semantic stereotype for it.

Mignucci's interpretation of the knowing definitely criterion is substantially correct as far as it goes, but it leaves out a crucial element. What we learn from Mignucci's experiment is that Aldous's private language may or may not coincide with public language and that the latter always remains the arbiter of semantic standards. But this does nothing to elucidate why it is that a paw or head can be known without reference to the body. As it stands, then, we are left with nothing more than the fact that that's the way things are.

5.4 Morales's Interpretation of the Knowing Definitely Criterion

Morales favors an equally semantic, but more objectual interpretation of the knowing definitely criterion. Morales claims that the principal feature of a genuine relative expression, "taller than," is its indefiniteness, and its need to be completed by a reference to some other thing. Ultimately, we rely on the meaning of the relative expression, Morales says, to indicate what the actual correlate should be. In every case, however, if a thing is to count as an *E* correlate it must exist and it must satisfy the conditions implied by the meaning of the relational word (Morales 1994, 263). Morales thinks the criterion involves knowing certain facts about an item as well as knowing the definition of the attribute. Morales makes no distinction, as does Mignucci (1986) of the difference between a definition and the meaning of an expression. Consequently, Morales thinks the epistemic requirements of the criterion will vary by case depending upon the meaning of the relational expression.

As I mentioned earlier in Chapter 2, Morales thinks that with E in particular, Aristotle is considering the necessary and sufficient conditions for the existence of concrete relative items. But Morales states that with the knowing definitely criterion, Aristotle is not concerned with what must be inferred from the existence of a relative but rather with the necessary conditions that must obtain if one is to know a relative. These conditions are almost exactly the conditions Mignucci adduces; namely, that both the relative and its correlative has appropriate grounds or subjects, and that the relational predicate be able to be truly predicated of the subject of the relative. Morales observes that Ackrill's counter-examples start from the assumption that a relative already exists. Ackrill's adopting this starting point means that the other minimal requirements for the existence of relational being are not considered in determining whether there exists something that stands related to the relative is a particular way.

Morales's Interpretation of the Substance Argument

For Morales, my knowing also involves knowing the definition of an item, e.g., knowing the definition of 'hand'. Aristotle says that one can know "that which is the ousia of such things" (i.e., heads and hands) (Categories 8b17). The meaning of ousia is notoriously ambiguous as it can mean "substance" or the "essence" of a thing. Either can be taken as implying the definition of a thing. For Morales, one's knowing also involves knowing the definition of an item, e.g., knowing the definition of hand.

Morales gives a plausible account of how the knowing definitely criterion and the completeness of substance words bolster Aristotle's argument to exclude substance from the category. Suppose, he suggests, that the definition of hand were "the part of the body that enables a living being to seize things to his advantage" (Morales 1994, 264). Morales explains that 'part' is the relational word needing further specification, not 'hand'. Since the definition of hand already includes the necessary completive reference, the term is definitionally complete. Such words are too complete or definite to count as genuinely relative expressions because they are not in need of completion.

Morales's argument, then, is as follows: Words whose definitions automatically include relational references to other words (i.e., the correlative word already contained in one word) are not true relatives (i.e., they are not *E* relatives). Now, the definition of a part word always contains a reference to its whole. For example, the hand is a part and the body is the whole. Thus, the definition of hand automatically contains a reference to the body. So, the parts of substance cannot be *E*-relative.

Morales is on the right track here. He refers the reader to Aristotle's stock example of "snub nose" at *Metaphysics* 1030b15–35, which I discussed earlier in Chapter 3. Aristotle states that certain words already contain a reference to their definition or definitional essence. Aristotle makes the same point at *Topics* 140b26–141a23. "Absurdity results," Aristotle contends, "not when the same word is uttered twice, but when the same thing is more than once predicated of a subject." The attribute of "snubness," Aristotle says, "is concavity in the nose. Since "snub" already contains a reference to "nose", to say that "a snub nose is a concave nose" would amount to saying the "same thing twice", i.e., "snub nose nose." So, to know the essence of the attributes such words name is to understand that the referenced item is already contained in them (see also *Topics* VI.3, 140b27–30, 141a2).

Morales argues that this is why it is not necessary to know the correlate in order either to know the definition of the object (i.e., the essence) or to recognize or otherwise know that the object is a hand (Morales 1994, 264). So, because 'head' and 'hand' are too definitionally or semantically complete to be in need of completion, they do not count as genuine relatives.

Morales argues that the epistemic demands of the criterion are not too strong. He also attempts to show how the distinction between indefinite (or "incomplete" as Ackrill puts it) relative expressions and definite (or complete) ones effectively prohibit secondary substances from the category of relatives.

I detailed above in Section 4.3 what I think are serious lapses in Morales's interpretation of the knowing definitely criterion with regard to his general analysis of Aristotle's relatives. Despite its lapses, though, Morales's analysis of the substance argument is the most reasonable and successful of the three. We can recap Morales's argument as follows: The parts of substances do not meet the knowing definitely criterion, and hence, are not relational because the substance can be defined without reference to the other part.

Morales's treatment presents Aristotle's epistemic demands for *E* and Aristotle's argument in a better light than does Ackrill's or Mignucci's. He finds a credible reason why there are different epistemic demands for relatives and non-relatives in the necessary indefiniteness of the former and the definiteness completeness of the latter. Because we rely on the meaning of the relational predicate to help us select the correlate, that meaning already includes as much semantic information about the referent and the correlate as we have in the case with complete expressions. But there is a difficulty here which Morales himself observes.

5.5 Why the Substance Argument Succeeds

One of the most perplexing things about Aristotle's description of relatives in *Categories* 7, is his claim that no substance is a relative. The reason why this is perplexing is that it forces us to grapple with the ontological dependence of these non-substantial entities. Primary substance, we know, has pride of place in Aristotle's ontology as the most real entities within the categories. If the *Categories* gives us a view of the kinds of "real" entities there are, then one would think that those genuine categorical entities are, in fact, concrete items. Does Aristotle want to have it both ways? Does he want to have relational items that are substances and at the same time exclude them from the category? Hardly. We should see Aristotle's work in laying out the categorial boundaries of the predicaments as proceeding first along metaphysical lines, then along existential lines. If we do this, then his concern here about substance makes more sense for it will be clear that what is being rejected is the notion that a substance could be one of the relational metaphysical predicates, not that substance is in no way involved with relational being.

Ammonius offers a good example of how the substance argument succeeds. Ammonius states: "Assume that Socrates has all the rest of his body covered, only a hand being exposed. In that case I know definitely that it is a hand even though I do not know definitely whose hand it is" (Cohen and Matthews 1992, 96).

In other words, we can point to the hand and ask, "What is the very thing that this is?" and not have to say whose hand it is. We can repeat the experiment with two bowls of ice cream—one with a single scoop, the other with double of that—it is impossible to tell whether that bowl of ice cream is double of the unseen and unknown one. This is not always the case, though. I might know that Café Pergolesi serves its double lattes in a particular size glass and its single lattes in another. I would not have to see both cups to know definitely that one was double of the other. My definite knowledge in this case depends upon memory, not on my perceiving both glasses simultaneously.

It is not the case that to be a head is to be a certain functional part of a living body of *someone*. Any body has a certain weight, but it is not the case that to be a head is to be a certain functional part of a living body of a certain weight. A head can be known definitely without reference to its complement, from Aristotle's perspective, precisely because of its functional unity with the body. To be a head, then, is to be a certain functional part of a body. Being a functional part of something is not the same as being a purely relational entity. A soldier may be a functional part of a regiment, but the soldier is not a purely relational entity. I can know definitely what a soldier is without having to know what identify the regiment of which the soldier is a part.

The same applies to a head. We have other means of knowing the very thing that a head is. For entities that are purely relational, on the other hand, we have no choice but to know them, so to speak, by the company they keep; i.e., by the items that are correlative to them.

This particular relational *aporia* is just one of the problems with Aristotle's relatives. In the end, perhaps Aristotle's extreme epistemic demands here are due to his overly strict sense that relation must be dyadic. It is inconceivable to him that there exists anything genuinely *E** relational without there being at least two items involved. Indeed, perhaps what the knowing definitely criterion shows most of all is that Aristotle believes, as do we, that relations are minimally dyadic in character.

As we have seen, none of the commentators gives a completely satisfactory account of the knowing definitely criterion and Aristotle's substance argument; nevertheless, each offers some important insight into Aristotle's solution to the *aporia*. Most important among these is seeing how in contrast to the incompleteness of relative expressions, substance words and substances themselves are too complete to be relational in the strict sense.

By taking seriously Aristotle's epistemological concerns in *Categories* 7, we find reasons to accept his solution to the *aporia*. The incompleteness of relative expressions discloses Aristotle's commitment to as dyadic a view of relations as his ontology will permit. What the force of the knowing definitely criterion proves is that Aristotle takes seriously the necessity to speak of genuine relatedness when at least two relatives stand in relation to one another. The seriousness of the view is indicated by the strength or, as some would say, the unreasonableness of the knowing definitely criterion.

5.6 Indefinite Relations and the Knowing Definitely Criterion

I turn now to the problem of reconciling the knowing definitely criterion of *Categories* 7 with the inclusion of indefinite numerical relations in *Metaphysics* V.15. In this Section I offer two reasons why Aristotle's positions in the *Categories* and in the *Metaphysics* may be viewed as compatible.

The problem of the compatibility of the knowing definitely criterion and indefiniteness of some numerical relations arises because on the one hand in *Categories* 7 Aristotle says relatives and their correlatives must always be known definitely, while on the other hand, according to *Metaphysics* V.15 numerical ratios can exhibit a degree of indeterminateness. One cannot resolve the problem by circumscribing the knowing definitely criterion so that it pertains to only non-numerical relations. Aristotle includes numerical relatives and their relations are part of those Aristotle includes in the *Categories* 7 account of relational being; hence, numerical relatives fall under the knowing definitely criterion.

Perhaps Aristotle has given up this epistemological criterion in the *Metaphysics* account. I mentioned in Chapter 3, that there are several differences between the *Categories* and *Metaphysics* accounts. One of those differences is that the knowing definitely criterion is dropped. This may have to do with the fact that the *aporia* over substance is no longer an issue. It may also be because Aristotle's meta-ontology is more developed and nuanced by the time of the *Metaphysics*. The fact that Aristotle would allow for the indeterminacy of relatives, especially with respect to numerical ratios, shows a more mature outlook on both relational and mathematical issues.

It is clear that we can use the knowing definitely criterion to determine whether definite numerical are relatives. If I know that this quantity of Ben and Jerry's ice cream is the double of a bowl with half as much ice cream, then I know that the ice cream in one bowl bears a 2:1 relation to the ice cream in the other bowl. But can the knowing definitely criterion reasonably be used to determine whether indefinite numerical relatives are genuinely relative?

In order for the criterion to be applicable to the indefinite numerical relations of *Metaphysics* V.15 we would have to modify our understanding of it slightly so it reflects what it means to know definitely an indefinite numerical relation. How would this work? We would need to be able to say that if a number is known to be relative to an unspecified number in an unspecified way, then this unspecified relationship must be known definitely. In other words, it could be known definitely that the numerical ratio in question is unspecifiable. This would mean affirming that the relation still exists in a particular way, even though that particular way cannot be specified precisely.

What could not be the case is thinking that the indefiniteness of the numerical ratio implies that there is no relation between the two terms. That is, we cannot take the fact that the term is unspecified as an indication that the correlative does not exist. This last option plainly has to be rejected because the fact that one term of the ratio is not specifiable does not mean that the ratio itself is not relational. The unspecified number makes it so that the relation between the two numbers can only be given in a rough way. Now this does not suggest that there is a number, *n*, such that we do not know at all whether it is elative to another number. Rather, all this means is that one definitely knows that the numerical relation is unspecifiable. None of the numerical relatives Aristotle discusses is so indefinite so as not to be related to a precise "something". As I noted earlier in Chapter 3, Aristotle considers these very indefinite numerical ratios unspecifiable because Aristotle does not recognize irrationals numbers as numbers. So, the "something" here which needs to be known definitely, is not a completely "unknown" entity. It term simply is not a number. While the above interpretation is removed somewhat from the original spirit of the knowing definitely criterion, I do not think it so far removed as to make the *Metaphysics* and *Categories* accounts incompatible on this issue of the knowing definitely criterion.

5.7 Summary

None of the commentators I have examined gives a completely satisfactory account of the definiteness criterion and Aristotle's substance argument; nevertheless, each offers some important insight into Aristotle's solution to the *aporia*. Most important among these is seeing how in contrast to the incompleteness of relative expressions, substance words and substances themselves are too complete to be relational in the strict sense.

In the end, perhaps Aristotle's extreme epistemic demands here are due to his overly strict sense that relation must be dyadic. It is inconceivable to him that there exists anything genuinely relational (i.e., *pros ti*) without there being at least two items involved. Indeed, perhaps what the definiteness criterion shows most of all is that Aristotle believes, as do we, that relations are minimally dyadic in character.

What the force of the knowing definitely criterion proves is that Aristotle takes seriously the necessity to speak of genuine relatedness when at least two relatives stand in relation to one another.

Chapter 6

Conclusion

The critics complain that for Aristotle's theory to count as a legitimate relational theory it must recognize the dyadic nature of relation. In order to demonstrate that Aristotle attempts to address this feature, we would have to find some evidence that he recognizes that there are at least two items, i.e., a dyad of items, involved in a relation, not just an accident or property being predicated of one item. Critics dismiss Aristotle's relational theory because they tend to think that the entities that inhabit the category of relation are of the same kind as the other predicaments: all the other non-substantial entities in the categories behave monadically, the relational ones must do so as well.

I believe Aristotle does all that he can do, given the constraints of his overall philosophical system, to argue, generally, that two specific items are necessary to have a relation. Aristotle pursues this theme with the vigor of a dogmatist in *Categories* 7. He insists that unless there are at least two items being related to each other in carefully prescribed ways, the relationality of the two items does not hold.

Aristotle uses the holding somehow component of *E* as a means of embracing the second thesis. The holding somehow component pinpoints and articulates something that acts not unlike a logical relational predicate. Simply put, Aristotle takes the holding somehow component to indicate how relational being involves a relation of at least two things to each other. The holding somehow component seems to foreshadow some third logical item, a relation, which holds the relative and correlative items of a relation together.

My purpose here has not been to defend Aristotle against all the supposed deficiencies of his relational theory, nor have I suggested that Aristotle was attempting to construct a theory comparable to our own. My point in bringing out the parallels between Aristotle's view and our own is not to be naively anachronistic, or to obscure the genuine limitations in Aristotle's relational theory. I agree that Aristotle does not have the logical apparatus to articulate our modern relational theory. Indeed, Aristotle's theory of relation cannot fit neatly into his own thinking about what constitutes a normative logical analysis (i.e., the subject-predicate analysis) of his ontology. However, notwithstanding the limitations of his other philosophical positions, Aristotle still manages to express a view of the dyadic nature of relation.

What Aristotle says about relatives shows that his thinking about relation is not as limited as Cornford, Russell and others suggest it is. After analyzing Aristotle's account of relatives and the crucial role they play in his conception of the category of relation, we have good reason to believe that Aristotle's views on relation are not as poverty-stricken as his critics would have us believe.

Notes

1. A few of Aristotle's most ardent critics are Cornford 1935, 283–284, Russell 1914, 33–59, and Weinberg 1965, 68–78.

2. Sometimes in Aristotle's logical treatises, he does use what passes for variables. See Mates 1972, 208. We find evidence of Aristotle's use of variables or quasi-variables throughout the *Prior Analytics* and *Posterior Analytics*. For typical instances see *Prior Analytics* 25a14 ff. and *Posterior Analytics* 72b8 ff.

3. Peggy the slave was my mother's grandmother's grandmother. Rachel the slave was my father's great-grandmother.

4. The history of the logic of modern relations begins with De Morgan 1847, De Morgan 1864, 331–358; Frege 1893, Peirce [1933] 1960, 195–206; and Russell and Whitehead 1927, Vol. I 200–202, 213, 228, 232.

5. Quine 1960, for instance, argues that the notion of attributes (e.g., slaveness) and relations (is a slave of) can be done away with, and that we can use sets or classes to articulate relations. Yet there is a sense in which the very notion of sets is fundamentally relational. Whether or not the members of a set are ordered pairs, whatever element or elements a set has in it, a set conveys a relation of *membership*. As Peter Simons observed at the 1992 SUNY Buffalo conference on Relation, since set theory is logically a theory of membership relation, set theory is implicitly relational and therefore relations cannot be avoided.

6. Some of the categories other than substance share certain characteristics belonging to another category, and thus fall within the scope of more than one category. See below, p. 134).

7. All translations are my own unless otherwise specified. Those not my own are taken, unless otherwise noted, from Jonathan Barnes, *The Complete Works of Aristotle*, The Revised Oxford Translation, ed. by J. Barnes, 2 vols., Princeton: Princeton University Press, 1984. Reference will be made to the individual translator only with page numbers omitted.

8. Any attribute is either predicable of a substance or present in a substance. If present in a substance, it I present in one substance at a time. Numerically one accident is, therefore, not in two subjects at a time. It is true that this is not *explicitly* stated. In Weinberg's view, Aristotle's account of the matter hardly allows another interpretation. The successors of Aristotle, he thinks, with some hesitation, at least in language, on the part of Simplicius and Al-Farabi, are in general agreement on this point. Thomas Aquinas, Avicenna, and Leibniz, for example, all deny that an accident can exist in two subjects at the same time. See Weinberg 1965, 75. For further discussion, see Henninger (1989).

9. Although the statements or propositions each share a similar surface structure ('*S* is *P*' or '*P* is said of *S*') and are all logically analyzable as F(*x*), they have different logical forms. (1) and (2) have a "said of" logical form, while (3) has an "inherence" logical form.

10. See Russell and Whitehead 1927, I. 291, 37.2 and 37.62. Wengert 1974, 165 n. 1 discusses the provenance of De Morgan's "horse" comment. He notes that the citation in the *Principia* refers to Jevons 1887, 18. Wengert reports that "Jevons says De Morgan used the example in conversation."

11. Throughout I shall use the word 'correlative' to refer to the relational attribute that stands in relation to a relative as its converse. For instance, the correlative for the relative <u>slave</u>, is <u>master</u>. Aristotle's ontology demands that every accident must have a subject in which it inheres or of which it is said. I will call the subject for a relative (or a correlative), the *ground* or *foundation* of the relative. The grounds of a relational pair are the *relata* of the relation. The ground of the relative is the *relatum*, the ground of the correlative is the *correlate*. The grounds of the relative-correlative pair constitute what normally would be for us the *logical terms* of a dyadic relation.

12. In addition to these properties of relations, Aristotle typically highlights the fact that relations have their converses. If R is any relation, we can define R′, the converse of R, by saying that for all x and all y, R′(xy) if and only if R(yx). For example, <u>smaller</u> and <u>larger</u> form converse relations: if x is smaller than y, then y is larger than x.

13. Dirk Baltzly cites Ammonius 70. 10–14, Porphyry 111. 28–29, Simplicius 159. 12–15, as well as Olympiodorus 112. 20 and David 215. 21 ff. See Baltzly 1997, 194.

14. Translation based on Pickard-Cambridge. The words in italics are mine. I substitute "of-something" for Pickard-Cambridge's "genitive." As Pickard-Cambridge notes, no words for grammatical terms appear in the Greek. See Barnes 1986, 209.

15. Aristotle expresses the same criterion is a slightly different way at *Topics* 142a26-31 and 146b3. There he says that it is impossible to know a relative without knowing its correlative.

16. Aristotle makes a similar point at *Rhetoric* 137a35. There he says that "anger must always be felt toward some particular individual, e.g., Cleon and not man in general."

17. Weinberg 1965, 74 also comments that calling them "cognitive," for instance, reflects the view of some medieval interpreters of Aristotle that these kinds of relations had one real term, i.e., (e.g., the thinkable), and one "rational" or mind-dependent term (e.g., thought).

18. Kirwan 1971, 165 notes the ambiguity in Aristotle's discussion of the sense of one here and at *Metaphysics* 1016b5–6, 8–9. He argues that since Aristotle allows two numerically distinct substances to count as being the same in species (e.g., the two books on my desk), Aristotle ought to consider two instances of the same color, say, the lemon's yellow (yellow1) and the legal pad's yellow (yellow2), as having not similarity, but some sort of specific or generic sameness.

19. See Kirwan's translation (Kirwan 1971, 52; italics mine). Ross's translation similarly reads: "For the thinkable implies that there *is* thought of it" (*Metaphysics* 1021a31, trans. Ross; italics mine).

20. See Gottlieb 1993 for a further examination of Aristotle's competing views of perception in connection with his account of relatives.

21. I have taken the liberty of using my own designations for the two definitions and relatives of each type ("*L*", "*L*-relative", "*E*", and "*E*-relative") in place of what Ackrill calls the first and second criterion.

22. Mignucci calls Aristotle's first definition of relational being "P1" and the second definition "P2" (see Mignucci 1986, 104, 106). For the sake of clarity and consistency, I have taken the liberty of using my own designations for the two definitions and relatives of each type ("*L*", "*L*-relative", "*E*", and "*E*-relative") in place of Mignucci's designations.

23. The exact formula Mignucci uses is:

$$\lambda x F(x) \ \varepsilon \ \text{P1} \ \textit{iff} \ \lambda x F(x) = \lambda x \exists y R F(x,y)$$

where 'P1' stands for what I have designated the *L* formulation of relational being and also the "class of relatives identified by Aristotle's definition" (Mignucci 1986, 104). The epsilon, 'ε', may be misused here. What Mignucci is trying to say is that the class of things that satisfy $F(x)$ is an element in the class of relatives that meets the first definition, *L*. The formula might better be off without the epsilon and rephrased:

$$F\text{-ness is a P1-relative } \textit{iff} \ \lambda x F(x) = \lambda x \exists y R F(x,y)$$

24. Morales identifies Aristotle's first and second definitions of relational being as "definition D1" and "definition D2". Once again, for the sake of clarity and consistency, I have taken the liberty of using my own designations ("*L*", "*L*-relative", "*E*", and "*E*-relative") in place of the commentator's designations.

25. According to *Topics* 121a5, a genus should fall under the same category as its species, but at *Categories* 11a20, Aristotle sanctions just the opposite. He describes the case mentioned here of the genus knowledge falling under one category and its species belonging to another. See Morales 1994, 265 and Ackrill 1963, 108-109 for further discussion of the difficulty.

26. Note that we find the being component of *E* nearly verbatim in the above italicized excerpt. The Greek at *Topics* 142a29, *tois toioutois tauton to einai tō pros ti pōs echein*, I would translate as before, emphasizing the holding somehow construction: "being for them is the *same as holding in some way toward something*."

27. I am adopting here a general approach suggested by Barry Smith at the 1995 SUNY Buffalo conference on Relation.

28. Although I here focus on the *Categories* 7 account, the schema presented applies to the relatives Aristotle treats in *Metaphysics* V.15. The names for capacity, intentional and incidental relatives still fall under the class of *L* relational entities; those same relatives understood as relational attributes correspond to *E* relational entities; and the actual relatives of each class correspond to E* relational entities.

Bibliography

Ackrill, J. L. 1963. *Aristotle's Categories and De Interpretatione.* Oxford: Clarendon Press.

Allen, R. E. 1969. "Individual Properties in Aristotle's Categories" *Phronesis* 24 (1): 31-39.

Ammonius *On Aristotle's Categories.* Trans by S. Marc Cohen and Gareth B. Matthews. Ithaca: Cornell University Press. 1992

Baltzly, Dirk. 1997. Plato, Aristotle, and the *logos ek ton pros ti. Oxford Studies in Ancient Philosophy* 15: 177-206.

Barnes, Jonathan. 1984, *The Complete Works of Aristotle,* The Revised Oxford Translation, ed. by J. Barnes, 2 vols., Princeton: Princeton University Press.

Cavarnos, Constantine. 1975. *The Classical Theory of Relations: A Study in the Metaphysics of Plato, Aristotle, and Thomism.* Belmont: Institute for Byzantine and Modern Greek Studies.

Cornford, F. M. 1934. *The Physics.* Loeb Classical Library Aristotle Vol. V. Cambridge: Harvard University Press.

_____. 1957. *Plato's Theory of Knowledge: The Theatetus and the Sophist of Plato.* New York: Macmillan Publishing Company.

De Morgan, Augustus. 1847. *Formal Logic, or The Calculus of Inference, Necessary and Probable.*

_____. 1864. On the Syllogism IV and on the Logic of Relations. *Cambridge Philosophical Transactions* 10: 331-358.

Edghill, E. M. 1928. *Categoriae and De Interpretatione.* Oxford: Oxford University Press.

Bibliography

Frege, Gottlieb. [1893] 1964. *Basic Laws of Arithmetic*, ed. by Montgomery Furth. Reprint. Berkeley: University of California Press.

Furth, Montgomery. 1988. *Substance, Form and Psyche: an Aristotelian Metaphysics*. Cambridge: Cambridge University Press.

Gottlieb, Paula. 1993. Aristotle versus Protagoras on Relatives and the Objects of Perception. *Oxford Studies in Ancient Philosophy* 11:101-119.

Heath, Thomas. 1949. *Mathematics in Aristotle*. Oxford: Clarendon Press.

Henninger, Mark G. 1989, *Relations: Medieval Theories 1250-1325*, Oxford: Clarendon Press.

Kirwan, Christopher. 1971. *Aristotle's Metaphysics, Books Γ, Δ, E.* Oxford: Clarendon Press.

Mates, Benson. 1972. *Elementary Logic*. New York: Oxford University Press.

Mignucci, Mario. 1986. Aristotle's Definitions of Relatives in *Cat.* 7. *Phronesis* 31: 101-127.

Minio-Paleullo, L. 1949. *Aristotelis Categoriae et Liber de Interpretatione*. Oxford: Clarendon Press.

Morales, Fabio. 1994. Relational Attributes in Aristotle. *Phronesis* 39: 255-274.

Owen, G. E. L. 1965. "Inherence." *Phronesis* 10: 97-105

Peirce, Charles. (1) [1933] 1960. "A Theory of Probable Inference." *Collected Papers of Charles Sanders Peirce*, Vol. III, ed. by Charles Hartshorne and Paul Weiss. Reprint, Cambridge: Harvard University Press.

_____. (2) [1933] 1960. "The Critic of Arguments." *Collected Papers of Charles Sanders Peirce*, Vol. III, ed. by Charles Hartshorne and Paul Weiss. Reprint, Cambridge: Harvard University Press.

Quine, Willard Van Orman. 1960. Word and Object. Cambridge, Mass.: The Technology Press of M.I.T

Ross, W. D. [1924a]. *Aristotle's Metaphysics*. Vol. 1. 1997. Sandpiper edition. Oxford: Clarendon Press.

_____. [1924b]. *Aristotle's Metaphysics*. Vol. 2. 1997. Sandpiper edition. Oxford: Clarendon Press.

Russell, Bertrand and Alfred North Whitehead. 1927. *Principia Mathematica*, 2nd ed. Cambridge: Cambridge University Press.

Russell, Bertrand. [1914]. *Our Knowledge of the External World*. 1993. Reprint, with an introduction by John Slater, London: Routledge.

_____.1959. *Problems of Philosophy*. Oxford: Oxford University Press.

Smith, J. A. 1921. "*Tode ti* in Aristotle." *Classical Review* 35.

Smyth, Herbert Weir. 1983. Greek Grammar. Cambridge: Harvard University Press, Revised edition.

Wedin, Michael V. 1993. "Nonsubstantial Individuals." *Phronesis* 38: 137-165

Weinberg, Julius R. 1965. *Abstraction, Relation, and Induction*. Madison and Milwaukee: The University of Wisconsin Press.

Index